The Sounds of Love and Grace

The Sounds of Love and Grace

TEN SOUNDS THAT WILL SAVE THE WORLD

Jimi Calhoun

CASCADE *Books* • Eugene, Oregon

THE SOUNDS OF LOVE AND GRACE
Ten Sounds that Will Save the World

Cascade Books
An Imprint of Wipf and Stock Publishers
199 W. 8th Ave., Suite 3
Eugene, OR 97401

www.wipfandstock.com

PAPERBACK ISBN: 978-1-5326-5814-3
HARDCOVER ISBN: 978-1-5326-5815-0
EBOOK ISBN: 978-1-5326-5816-7

Cataloguing-in-Publication data:

Names: Calhoun, Jimi, author.

Title: The sounds of love and grace : ten sounds that will save the world / Jimi Calhoun.

Description: Eugene, OR: Cascade Books, 2020 | Includes bibliographical references.

Identifiers: ISBN 978-1-5326-5814-3 (paperback) | ISBN 978-1-5326-5815-0 (hardcover) | ISBN 978-1-5326-5816-7 (ebook)

Subjects: LCSH: Ten Commandments. | Christian life. | Race relations.

Classification: BV4655 .C23 2020 (print) | BV4655 (ebook)

Manufactured in the U.S.A.   JANUARY 7, 2020

Dedication

In memory of Charles and Mark Hemphill,
G. Michael and Samantha Lawrence, Travis Tanner, Riley Webb,
Jean Macaluso, Lynn New, William Thomas Murphy,
Katie Graham, and Marilyn Bellucci.

Dedicated to William and Xanthyne Calhoun
and Jules and Lorraine Brown.

Table of Contents

Preface

Listen Here—Hear, Listen!

THIS IS A BOOK about the Ten Commandments. It is intended to be an application of them and not an explanation of them. The Macmillan Dictionary states that the phrase *Listen Here* "is used when you want someone to pay attention to what you are saying."[1] The primary ask of this book is that you would consider doing what Jesus asked of his followers centuries ago, "Listen carefully to what you hear!"[2] The reason this book is needed at this time is amplified by this quote from the great philosopher and poet Henry David Thoreau: "If a man does not keep pace with his companions, perhaps it is because he hears a different drummer. Let him step to the music which he hears, however measured or far away."[3]

When it comes to race, disability, immigration, religious intolerance, and political division, there are many in our society that have not kept pace with the shifting landscape of the world around them. This has resulted in increased social segregation, even isolation, for a large number of people. I invite you to hear the beat of that different drummer by "re-listening" to ten drumbeats from a distant past. The distant past I am referring to dates back to the time when Moses first heard the Ten Words from God on Mount Sinai, thousands of years ago.

1. Macmilliandictionary.com/, "Listen."
2. Mark 4:24 CEV.
3. Brainyquote.com/, "Thoreau."

ix

How to Read This Book

When I studied for the ministry, students were taught that the teachings of Jesus were best understood when their historical context was taken into consideration. I believe the same holds true about what Moses taught, part of which were the Ten Commandments, or the Ten Words. This book is written with the understanding that Judaism and Christianity were born under the same figurative roof. Although they have each carved out separate and independent rooms, they are closer to being siblings than rivals. I have quoted several scholars and rabbis from the Jewish tradition to help us interpret these Ten Commandments through the world view of the tradition into which they were given. I have capitalized the words Ten and Words when speaking of The Ten Commandments, and Word when speaking of a single Commandment.

I suggest that you read the following chapters as you would enjoy a musical performance. That means you approach the Ten Words to experience them rather than to analyze them. When someone attends a concert, he or she wants to hear and feel the music—that is why a person dances whenever the music touches the soul. Portions of the subject matter I address in this book may be somewhat difficult to hear. For that reason, I encourage you beforehand to listen with an empathic ear and then place yourself at the scene of those stories that may be troublesome.

The Oxford Dictionary says that to listen is to "give one's attention to a sound,"[4] and the Cambridge Dictionary defines a sound as "how something seems to be, from what is said or written."[5] Encyclopedia.com defines a sounding as, "information or evidence ascertained as a preliminary step before deciding on a course of action."[6] I hope this book gives you a fresh sounding on the Ten Commandments, which are the foundation of a good and just social order. The sounds that you will hear on these pages are not political and should not be interpreted as such—they are spiritual, sociological, philosophical, and theological. Please sit back, open your heart, and then enjoy listening to what I call the sounds of love and grace.

4. Lexico.com/, "Listen."
5. Dictionary.cambridge.org/, "Sound." Sec. 9 (Seem).
6. Encyclopedia.com/, s.v., "Soundings," line 3.

Acknowledgments

THIS BOOK EXISTS DUE to the encouragement and the unwavering faithfulness of my wife, Julaine Catherine Calhoun.

And as a result of the many family members who have been there throughout the journey. I thank you and love you.

I am grateful for the support of those who have believed in me and have understood that the best instrument for connecting what is divided is a bridge. These include Robert, Kimberly, and Ian Watson-Hemphill, Kenneth and Lorraine Hoffman, Scott Varneau, Kate Gupta, Stanley and Maureen Ermeav, and Rudy and Leanne Greene.

I would like to acknowledge those who have made contributions to this book through their love, encouragement, and support over many years: Mary K. Shanahan, Kathie Lawrence, Ralph and Ruby Moore, Zac and Julie Nazarian, Alan and Mary Kisaka, Paul Louis Metzger, Paul Kraus, Sterling and Janie Spell, Bryan, Blair, and Daniel Anderson, Nicole and Donnie Christenson, Steve Kinney, Mike Adams, Cynthia Caruso, Marvin Jones, Ed and Patti Woolery-Price, Stephen Woolery-Price, the Doyal Family, my small group families, Wade Sullivan and Susan Thomas, Shannon Sedwick, Winston Williams, Brian Joseph, Gavin Lance Garcia, John T. Wright, Ryan Redfern, Terri Lynn Raridon, Debbie Russell, Luis Zapata, Heather Carraher, Rodney Clapp, Savanah Landerholm, and Hannah Harris.

A heartfelt thank you to my musical family, which has not only inspired me but taught me how to listen: Clifford Coulter, Jerry Perez, Ron E. Beck, Leon Patillo, Carol Stallings, Neil Stallings, Dennis Marcellino, Joseph Provost, Lenny Goldsmith, Dennis Kenmore, Eddie Tuduri, Clark Baldwin, Victor and Patricia Behm, Sydney George, Travis Fullerton, Napoleon Brock, Roy Vierra, Arturo Chavez, Renaldo Guzman, Louis Oros, Jimmy McGhee, Johnny Rocker, Connie Jones, Gloria Scott, Bill and Ruth

ACKNOWLEDGMENTS

Carter, Gabe Rhodes, John Fannin, Linda Scott, Danny and Debi Brooks and Lynn Daniel, Freddy Staehle, Fred Mandujano, and Wayne Rediker.

I would also like to acknowledge the friends who have helped shape who I am: the Ingram family; Walter Huddleston; Peter and the Shiver family; Francis and the Tanner family; Willie, John, and the Scott family; the Urias family; Richard and the Gonzales family; Albert Lopez; Alfred Hernandez; Joe, Cheryl, and the Gallo family; Gabriel, Vince, and the Strangis family; Jane Macaluso; Edaordo Imperial; Nancy Zerkas; Marie Maes Munley; Dennis and Cleo Barone; Dave and Don Conley; Jim Guido; Mike Goodman; Jim Heckendorn; Joe Spatafore; Brad Gardner; and Jeanne and Elle Adams.

I

An Introduction

What Is Soul?

PHILOSOPHER MARTIN BUBER SAID this about the Ten Commandments: "Their task is to call forth man's response to the Divine, the response of the complete human being, and hence, the unification of the spiritual and the worldly."[1] Sounds wonderful right? But how? Throughout these pages, I will argue that Mr. Buber's vision for a holistic understanding of the Commandments is the launchpad for strengthening our moral convictions and the ethical practices they produce, through a process of internal listening. I understand that "listening" to printed words may not be what immediately comes to mind when the word *listen* is used—but as a former professional musician, I can assure you that it is possible. Here is why.

Music is fundamentally information in the form of sounds or notes. In order to become proficient at playing an instrument, a musician must develop the means to access the information for use in performance. The majority of rock and funk musicians learn their craft through the process called playing by ear. They listen to musical information, internalize what they have heard, and then use it to produce music. The music they produce is the result of note patterns stored in a type of musical cache through years of listening and practicing. I am suggesting that this process is similar to what we do when we read a book, only we use our sense of sight to access information. When we read a book we visually access information, and

1. Buber, *On Judaism*, 169.

1

then utilize our memories to store the ideas for future use. I am asking that you emulate a rock or funk musician and access the "notes" written on these pages, then listen to the concepts in this book via the ears of your heart.

Rabbi Jonathan Sacks said of the Ten Commandments, "The Torah calls them *aseret hadevarim*, that is, 'ten utterances.' Hence the Greek translation, *Decalogue*, meaning 'Ten Words.'"[2] An *utterance* is a verbal sound, and this book assumes that a variety of sounds come at each of us from external sources as well as internal, and that those sounds have an effect on our behavior. For example, the sounds of nationalism, cultural identity, and even our family's values contribute to the attitudes that shape who we are and the choices we make. In the Talmud Rav Hananel bar Pappa said, "What is the meaning of that which is written? *Listen*, for I will speak royal things."[3]

Notice that what is spoken illumines and interprets what is written. Prior to the printing press knowledge was transferred orally and not visually. The spoken word preceded the written word and people worked hard to improve their listening skill in much the same way that we develop our reading skill today. Listening properly has become a lost art very much in need of being retrieved. Listening is a process through which we can reset our internal ethical and moral default systems and make better decisions. Rabbi Sacks also said, "Whether between us and God or us and other people, listening is the prelude to love."[4]

I will argue in the following pages that people spend a fair amount of time listening to those non-musical "sounds" just mentioned, in addition to a host of others. There are many scientists who believe that the ear can receive data that the conscious brain has difficulty understanding, and I contend that the same holds true for the ears of our souls. So this chapter is not so much of an introduction as it is an invitation. I am inviting you to listen to the lyrics of the ten sounds of morality and ethics given to Moses on Mount Sinai, and to listen in a completely different way. Many of us limit our listening to what will align with our biases. At that point we become willing listeners to things such as self-help talks, advice from politicians, and even gossip from friends, without ever considering the impact those

2. Sacks, *Essays on Ethics*, 104.

3. Davidson, "Talmud" para. 3, line 12.

4. Sacks, "Spirituality of Listening," para. 18, line 1.

sounds have on the way we understand the world. Here is the strongest statement I will make in this book: If you think, you have biases.

Listening is a means of accessing and unlocking subconscious biases in ways that simply thinking about something is unable to. I am suggesting that it is in everyone's best interest to become as discriminating about the words listened to as we are about what foods go into our bodies. This book is written in partial agreement with Greek philosopher Aristotle who wrote, "The soul neither exists without a body nor is a body of some sort. For it is not a body, but it belongs to a body, and for this reason is present in a body, and in a body of such-and-such a sort."[5] He also said, "The soul is the cause (*aition*) of life . . . the soul is the cause and principle of the living body."[6] The question that may need answering before we enter into our discussion about listening is what is the thing called the *soul*?

Let us start with an observation about the soul attributed to Charles Darwin by social anthropologist Christopher Boehm in his book *Moral Origins*. "His [Darwin's] treatment of self-conscious conscience was particularly provocative because now he was bringing his naturalistic approach close to the soul, previously the exclusive purview of the church, or more precisely God. Darwin did not take on the problem of how human beings came to have a soul."[7] Rather than scouring scientific or theology books to get ideas about the soul, I decided to use a completely different research tool for a launching pad: Facebook. On Facebook I asked friends to respond to the question, "What is Soul?" Several friends chimed in. The layout for the remainder of this chapter will consist of an answer from my friends in italics, followed by a brief commentary from me. I use the word *commentary* to describe my responses because they are designed to contextualize my friends' answers in relation to what this book is about. Each section will begin with a restating of the question, "What is Soul?" then a response, and then finally a comment by me. I have used a capital S when referring to Soul as a music form, and the culture that surrounds it. And I have used a lower-case s when referring to the human soul.

Here we go.

5. Cowen, "Aristotle on the Soul," section 4, line 3.
6. Cowen, "Aristotle on the Soul" (PsycheDisplay.pdf), section 4, line 22.
7. Boehm, *Moral Origins*, 7.

What is Soul?

Motown, Mr. James Brown, Aretha Franklin, Four Tops, Temptations, Sam Cooke, Little Stevie Wonder, Curtis Mayfield, and so many more . . . and that's the music of my soul.

Soul as music:

I am an author, ethicist, and musician living in Austin, Texas. Austin is a city that is affectionately nicknamed "the live music capital of the world." Here is why this is relevant. I am also an ordained minister in the Christian tradition, but I once earned my living by playing bass guitar with internationally known musical groups. One style of music that I played was called "Soul Music." Some of the artists I performed with as a bassist include the Four Tops, Lou Rawls, Etta James, and another Motown star named Martha Reeves, of "Dancing in the Street" fame. I also recorded and toured with a Soul singer named Gene Redding, and while he never achieved national acclaim, his vocal ability certainly warranted it.

Allow me to set the stage for what follows with something found in a song that my band named Gene Redding and Funk recorded. The song contained a type of "call and response," with the call coming in the form of a question, "What is Soul?" Although the question was rhetorical in the song, it sets the stage to provide an answer to the next question. Where is the information that we use to make decisions about right and wrong stored? It is kept in that inner place of knowing called the soul!

Shortly after the song "Soul" was released, I participated in a tour with the band. That string of dates began in Los Angeles and included the states of Oregon, Washington, and Idaho, before I made my way home to the San Francisco Bay area. Every night we would end our show with the song *I Got Soul*. I remember Gene belting out lyrics that rhetorically asked the people dancing why their lifestyles were as they were. They went something like this: "Why do you be doing the things you be doing when you be doing it?" In the true call-and-response style of the era, the answer came in the form of, "Shucks I don't know, but one thing I know is, I got Soul!" Ah, yes, Gene had Soul, the guitarist Jimmy McGhee had Soul, I had Soul, as did a fair number of the members of the listening audience. Had we needed to describe that thing we held in common it would have been very difficult, because "Soul" was indefinable.

4

The word *Soul* may have been indefinable in a musical sense, but we accepted that whatever it was, we knew that it shaped who we were and how we viewed life. Today, many people like to believe that each of us is in possession of some form of an inner compass that points us in the right direction as we live our lives. Do you believe that an innate moral compass exists? Perhaps it would be good for you to join in the chorus from Gene's song and internally sing, "Shucks I don't know!" I am aware that "I don't know" is not a very satisfying answer for those who desire certainty. However, for those of you who are comfortable with mystery, it is the perfect answer.

What is Soul?

True soul is like love, something you can't see but you can feel when you're in the midst [of it].

Soul as a state of being:

For Gene Redding and Funk, Soul was simply "a thang!" It was an indescribable entity from within that expressed our feelings and made a statement that we were in solidarity with other Soulful people. Soul also defined what type of musicians we were. When we would play that funky, funky Soul music, the dancers could not mistake us for jazz players, rock players, folk players, or even classical musicians. We were just a foot-stomping, perspiration-inducing dance band that made everyone want to get on the floor and move. In this instance Soul was the impetus for the hearers to get their bodies in step with the pulsating thump of my bass and Joe's drums, and then shake like there was no tomorrow. At the end of the day, the answer to what is really an ontological question, "What is Soul?," cannot be anything other than, "Shucks I don't know, but it makes you be feeling good, oh yeah!"

What is Soul?

The holistic sum total of an entire human being i.e., body, mind, and spirit in one integrated whole.

Soul as personhood:

If Soul music is an "unknowable thang" as Gene Redding put forward, then is it possible the human soul is too? The philosopher Plato was a dualist and that led him to the belief that the body and soul were two separate entities, but he seemed to be curious as to how that worked. He believed that the soul was unchanging and that it was external to the body while also residing in it—so his dualism was a bit of a mystery. Plato also believed the soul to be immortal. He appeared to believe that the soul, related to our internal essence, consisted of three elements; a) how we think, b) what we desire, and c) the passions that drive us. His student Aristotle disagreed, and believed that the body and soul were inseparable, making them indivisible parts of a human being. For him the soul was simply the composite of those two entities working in tandem to make a person who they are.

Right about now you may be asking yourself, "What am I expected to make of what was just said? Haven't we veered off the Soul music course a little?" Well, yes and no. What was just mentioned is called a duality in philosophy. One of the ways dualities come into play is when something is described as a divided "whole." We are able to see dualities as complementary, but at other times we see them as opposites. A good example would be the way we have referred to a male and female as being members of the opposite sex—but we would hardly ever refer to the other side of a coin as an opposite. That is because it is understood that a male and female, while both human beings, are separate from each other, while a coin is a single entity with two sides.

Moses descended Mt. Sinai carrying two tablets, and each one had a set of instructions that were not opposites but complementary. The first set of Commandments dealt with the way we are to relate to God, meaning morality. The second set laid out the way we are to relate to each other, meaning ethics. We should not hear these Words as bifurcated beats allowing for a choice in which set to dance to, meaning to obey—we should instead hear them in stereo. Soul music needs two players, a bassist and a drummer, working together to make it funky. By analogy, the pursuit of a spiritual life needs two players, morality and ethics, to keep us honest and real. The place where the work is done in developing the mind and heart to be capable of hearing what is honest and real is the soul. When a Christian's love for others becomes equal to their love for God, that is when they will know that they have listened correctly. That is also when they will dance to that funky, and spiritual, Soul music just the way they should.

Derek Parfit writes, "We should reject a moral theory if it is in this sense unrealistically demanding."[8] Would that suggest we should only accept a moral theory if we can execute it comfortably? We know that living up to high moral standards often comes with restrictions we perceive to be constraints, making them seem impractical. The truth is, to consistently behave in an ethical manner can actually be impractical and even draining. That is why many choose to skirt ethics. However, we cannot form a society that is just without a moral code, and never-ending human conflict is the fruit of unethical behavior. I am convinced that, pragmatism aside, we need morality and ethics to survive as a race.

To help resolve any tension that might come from defining morals and ethics separately, I ask that you see them as functionally similar to the concepts represented by the Chinese symbols of yin and yang. The online resource Wikipedia says yin-yang is "a concept of dualism in ancient Chinese philosophy, describing how seemingly opposite or contrary forces may actually be complementary, interconnected, and interdependent in the natural world."[9] The meaning behind the symbols has to do with the existence of a harmonious relationship between two objects and not a competition between, or an opposition to, the other. And that is exactly the way I see the two tablets given to Moses, and the moral and ethical codes emblazoned on them functioning in our lives.

What is Soul?

That which makes a person unique—the intangible, untouchable, unknowable essence emanating from God/Source/Universe/one.

Soul as spirit:

I recorded an album titled *Do It Now* with a jazz musician named Clifford Coulter. In one song he raised a very interesting question: why was he Clifford and not somebody else? A recent scientific experiment involving chimpanzees sought to learn whether or not chimps would know who they were if they looked into a mirror. Pop superstar Michael Jackson once sang about having to deal with "the man in the mirror," challenging himself to

8. Parfit, *Reasons and Persons*, 29.
9. Wikipedia, "Yin Yang," line 1.

reflect on his character. I imagine another question could be, "What makes you you?" The personal characteristics people acquire along the path of life matter very little in deciding what type of person you are in a biological sense. While writing this section I thought about bioethics because of an article I had read that very week about an operation that was to take place in China. It was represented to be the world's first "head transplant." The idea of a head being transplanted is so out of the norm that I decided to provide a link to the story below.[10]

As I read the article, I wondered why the writer characterized it that way. The operation entailed the surgeons connecting a head to a body and so why not a total body transplant? Should these types of operations become commonplace, will doctors match skin color before going forward? As race conscious as we are in America, and as litigious as we are, I can see some major lawsuits on the horizon. What happens if the doctors were to use the head of a person from a different racial group than the body? Just think, how would a person with a white head and black body be classified in a census?

If you are someone who believes that race defines the type of person someone is, that scenario should force you to revisit the question, what is the actual makeup of a person? Is it the body, or is it the soul, that makes a person real? In a very tragic sense, most Americans believe it is not the soul that makes someone who they are, it is the body and the racial body at that. However, anyone who has danced to that funky, funky Soul music would probably argue that the true makeup of a person is situated in the soul. Let us end these musings with this thought: many scientists say that our sense of self, or the soul, is located in the right frontal lobe of our brain. However, Gene Redding would put it this way: "No matter where you get it, you gotta have it." That's Soul.

What is Soul?

A type of food that is made with love, beans, and grits. I. E. Chicken and Waffles and fried okra.

---

10. Scienceinsanity.com, "World's First Human Head Transplant."

Soul as sustenance:

I read about a British teenager whose diet consisted of nothing but chicken nuggets for more than fifteen years. She occasionally extended her diet to include toast or potato chips, but for the most part, it was pretty much a mono-diet. A mono-diet, sometimes called a monotropic diet, is a diet that consists of a single source of nutrition. That could be a picture that illustrates the way many of us live out our faith. A fresh listen to the Commandments should result in a broader and more balanced understanding of what it means to be a Christian. We have a responsibility to be empathetic and compassionate in many different ways, and a mono-spiritual diet will not fill the bill. Justice for the marginalized should not be held in abeyance because all of our spiritual energy is expended on personal piety. This book is written with the understanding that human beings were made with love, to give love, and anything short of that is an ethical failure on our part.

What is Soul?

Your innermost elements.

Soul as an essential:

That answer said to me that the soul is *the* defining part of who we are. To be human is to have a soul and to have a soul is to be human. To be human also includes the capacity to be both moral and ethical and to pursue the common good. A lifestyle dedicated to the pursuit of the common good is broader and more complex than simply a matter of right and wrong. That is because people from different cultures often disagree about what justice is. It is the soul that generates both the vision for, and the power to, do good—even when our brains are begging us to move in the opposite direction.

How is it that we came to be human according to the Bible story? God breathed into us, and we became "living souls." The Jewish morning prayer says, "My Lord, the soul you gave me is pure. You created it, you formed it inside of me, you breathed into me."[11] The soul testifies to the goodness of God and the intention of God to bring that same kind of goodness out of us. The idea that we have access to that "power of goodness" should be true across all cultures and faith traditions because of who God is. Being special

11. Derrida, *Acts of Religion,* 164.

to God should give us a reason to join in and sing the words Gene would sing every night, "Sho makes you be feeling good, oh yeah!"

What is Soul?

The snow casting a shadow on the ground, blanketing our presence in its radiance while guiding our perceptions into the wonder of holiness.

Soul as light:

In his book *Eclipse of God*, Martin Buber recalled a conversation he had about a certain type of listening. It required that a person listens as "one who really wished to hear"[12] all that was being said. Early in my career as a Christian minister I used cognitive skills to interpret the Ten Words. That resulted in me seeing them only as rules or laws. I did not listen to them incorrectly or even improperly, I simply engaged them the way most people in my faith tradition did. The commentaries I read offered different explanations for how to, and why we should reach one conclusion about the Ten Words if we only thought about them correctly. Once I learned to listen to them using my heart like a set of headphones, I have been able to understand them quite differently.

The Hebrew word *shema* means to hear or listen. Part of the definition for the word *shema* includes the idea of paying attention in order to understand. Listening is learning and learning paves the way for understanding. The Hebrew verb *haazinu* means to give ear or hear, and the verb *tishma* means to listen. It has been put this way: "These separate verbs in Hebrew, *haazinu* and *tishma,* are synonyms on the surface, but reflect nuances in their different definitions. *Haazinu* refers to the physical act of hearing."[13] But the verb "*tishma* calls us forward to listen, obey, and understand at once."[14] In that light, consider the *Shema*: "Hear, O Israel, the LORD our God, the LORD is one" (Deut 6:4). The *Shema* is based on the latter verb (*tishma*) for listening, and that understanding has enabled me to interpret the Ten Words in a completely different way. I never imagined these Commandments could relate to so many areas of life when I thought of them

---

12. Buber, *Eclipse of God*, 4.
13. Goldstein, "On Hearing and Listening," line 12.
14. Goldstein, "On Hearing and Listening," line 16.

only as "the law." Now that I have listened to them through a different set of ears, I know it is possible for peace and justice to prevail in our lives provided we are willing to listen to the right things in the right way.

I write with the belief that each of us can develop the level of listening skill sufficient to improve our ability to hear from God. I am speaking of a type of listening that continues even in environments of complete silence. Scientists have known for quite a while about the reality of silent music, and inaudible sound, and my use of the concept is neither original nor new. British Neurologist Oliver Sacks suggested in the preface to his book *Musicophilia* that we construct music in our minds by using many parts of our brains. Mr. Sacks pointed out, "Listening to music is not just auditory and emotional, it is motoric as well. 'We listen with our muscles' as Nietzsche wrote."[15]

Recently I was surprised to learn that a fifth grader named Nick Penna had grasped the power of this type of listening. He wrote in a poem, "Your ears don't always listen, it can be your brain, your fingers, your toes, you can listen anywhere."[16] Psalm 81:13 cries out for those who follow God to listen where it says, "If my people would only listen."[17] Best-selling author Lynne McTaggart said, "'Listen' with your five senses, pay attention to the smell, taste, and kinesthetic feel of a situation."[18] The idea of actionable listening is real, and it is why I am confident that the sound of words, both the silent and audible variety, can become tools for loving—and that is the objective—learning to love by listening. As you begin to re-listen to the Ten Commandments, please understand that they contain the timeless social vision of our God.

What is Soul?

The intersection of the human and divine, the seat of our morals and ethics, and the sounds of love and grace.

15. Sacks, *Musicophilia*, 12.
16. Fox, *Poetic Medicine*, 96.
17. Ps 81:13, NIV.
18. McTaggart, *The Bond*, 223.

2

Belonging

I Am the Lord Your God, You Shall Have No Other Gods before Me (Exod 20:2–3).

MARTIN BUBER WROTE, "HE who decides with all his soul decides for God."[1] Every society has understood the need to develop some sort of moral code by which to ground the ethical behavior of its citizens. Where do you believe that the go-to resource for moral guidance is located in today's "post-everything" culture? Rabbi Jonathan Sacks wrote that one of the possibilities can be found in the covenant between the Jewish people and God, "For it aims at nothing less than the construction of a society that would moralize its members, inspire others, and serve as a role model of what might be achieved."[2]

When I have shared a similar idea, I have been accused of holding on to a naïve, idealistic, and impractical vision for saving the world. Guilty! That frees me to further state that saving the world includes saving it from the many competing versions of morality that have produced so much conflict between nations, cultures, and races. A morality that can save us from ourselves must originate outside of political, legal, or even religious institutions. This type of morality is rooted in covenant. Covenant is the glue that cements the concept of belonging that we will discuss in this chapter,

---

1. Buber, *On Judaism*, 66.
2. Sacks, "The Book of the Covenant," para. 16.

because unlike a contract, there are no performance clauses required to receive the benefits attached.

There were two heroic souls in the Hebrew Scriptures named Abraham and Moses that decided for God. Their decisions resulted in a covenant relationship with God like the one under discussion here. When thinking about what a covenant relationship might look like, picture what it would mean for you to be a committed ally with someone. The Oxford Dictionary defines *ally* as one who works to "combine or unite a resource with (another) for mutual benefit."[3] Consider the traditional marriage covenant as it was understood in Western culture. It was expected that once the wedding vows were sealed, one party would give up their surname in a show of total commitment to the union. Lately, many couples have decided to combine their surnames, not as a break with tradition, but as an enhancement of it. In my view, hyphenated last names signal that each person is respectful of their partner's roots, and so they see the joining of their names as an addition. Roots matter, and as we will see later, they matter a lot.

As we move forward please keep the words *mutual* and *benefit* close at hand. Abraham was involved in a covenant relationship with God, initiated by his willingness to listen to God, and then embark on a completely new adventure with God. This allegiance, sealed through covenant, assured Abraham that he and his family belonged to God. The covenant God made with Moses was similar in nature, but over time the number of principles involved expanded.

The relationship between God and Moses produced a covenant between God, Moses, and the people of Israel. It was codified through Moses on Mount Sinai when he received what is called the Ten Words. The Mosaic covenant was given within earshot of all the people of Israel, which made it a covenant of inclusion from its inception. I ask that you interpret the opening stanza of The Ten Commandments as being more about God's love for all that are "his," rather than simply God identifying himself as the person having the right to tell us what we should or should not do. For the remainder of this book please view the Ten Words as gifts from God that give us direction and meaning rather than laws to violate.

My sensitivity to the word *belonging* began as I grew up a minority youth who often "longed to be" included by the majority culture. That longing occurred during a time when most people in the majority culture believed that I had no inherent right to belong. However, the opening words

3. Oxforddictionaries.com, "Ally (verb)," line 1.

of the first Commandment say "your God" to everybody, and that phrase signals equal access to all. For most of my life people in the majority culture have lived as though the words really meant "their God," and any covenant-derived blessing attached was directed at them. But belonging in our context is made evident through welcome, acceptance, and full membership. It becomes actualized when people are aware that you not only belong to God as individuals, but you are connected with a host of others and belong together. That includes the people that you have always referred to as "them." When we fully understand that grace connects us to God's love for all, rather than our racial heritage, then social interaction with "others" that are equally connected by grace will come naturally.

Unfortunately, the Western bent towards racial pride and individualism plays a different song and its lyrics produce societal dissonance. In the 1970s teen icon Rick Nelson sang that if you can't please everyone then you might as well please yourself. That is how we roll, right? If you are smart you will put yourself first. Extending yourself for the good of another simply because it might be the right thing to do is deemed rubbish. However, there were two men in the Hebrew Scriptures named Abraham and Moses who did just that when they decided for God. Every day of our lives we are forced to make decisions. Decisions like, who it is that I should welcome, and who it is I should reject. Who should we accept as being like ourselves, and who are "those people"? Reflecting on the covenants that God made with these two giants of faith can help us with our decision-making processes. Hopefully, that leads us to develop a better appreciation for Abraham and Moses, and that will cause us to decide for God just as they did. A realization that each of us belongs to God and to each other is the starting point for both morality and ethics.

In reference to a Jewish Seder, Shabbat 88b reads, "God's voice at Sinai was heard in every language."[4] This is important for two reasons. The first is that it seems to suggest that the people of Israel were multicultural from their earliest days. Second, the need for people following God to be inclusive was factored in from the beginning. One of the ways white Christians have historically marginalized darker-skinned Christians is to question their spiritual roots. Ideally, every Christian would know that their tradition is rooted in the words God spoke to Moses. But since so many Bible teachers have relegated the Torah to almost second-class status by labeling

---

4. Dickson, *Gospel of Moses*, 29.

it "the Old Testament," many in our churches are ignorant about their spiritual heritage.

What's the Difference?

Roots matter and this is why. Many white Christians look down their noses at the worship style of people in black churches, and then justify their negative attitudes by labeling the roots of their spirituality as being backward, superstitious, and certainly un-Christian. These Christians believe that their God would never see *those* people as equal partakers in what God was doing in *their* lives. They are not racists necessarily—they simply assume that God is blessing their race, their country, etc. Let me illustrate that attitude outside of a church or religious context. Country music lovers enjoy what is called line dancing. The majority of people involved in this type of dance wear cowboy hats and are white. Line dancing is culturally accepted and is not believed to be vulgar, even among the majority of white evangelicals. However, when black people dance in a line to a different kind of music called hip hop, dancing becomes vulgar and a sign of much worse.

That becomes the justification for some white people to maintain a safe distance from those culturally repugnant people. That attitude surfaces in the church where the differences in liturgical style between black and white people on Sunday morning is enough reason to worship separately. Add to that the derogatory myths people invent about those mysterious others and the perfect storm for social segregation is formed. Social segregation is the love child of legal segregation's union with voluntary self-segregation. John Powell observed that "the civil rights movement has been successful in opening up public spaces (for blacks) just in time to see power and privilege (for whites) shift to private spaces."[5] This is the type of segregation where people are quite comfortable with the understanding that life is best lived in racially insulated spaces—in this instance the church. Social segregation in churches also results in theological dualisms that slice God in two disparate halves with each half having little in common with the other.

Theological dualism causes people that attend self-segregated churches to believe they have little in common with the God that is worshiped at those "other" churches. God becomes the mechanism for segmentation within the church instead of a unifying sign for it. If you doubt this, please ask yourself when was the last time you made an effort to attend a church

5. Powell, "Whiteness and Spatial Racism," para. 4, line 1.

whose attenders were from a racial group different than yours. Then ask yourself how many times have you visited a faith community made up of attendees from a different racial group in order to befriend someone. How many times have you attended one of those types of churches with the hope of one day belonging to it? Now ask yourself why.

Oh My God!

The first Commandment ends with a warning against paying attention to other gods, and by doing so, it tacitly acknowledges the existence of other gods. Who were those gods? I am going to paraphrase Bob Dylan for one possible answer: "There are many here among us who think God is but a joke." Throughout history people have invented deities to provide for their perceived needs. Though they may not have taken God seriously, they took the idea of having gods very seriously and so they made some up. Consider a few brief examples of the false gods from around the ancient world. People created gods to explain and justify their lived realities. Their lives centered around gender hierarchies, inter-royal-familial rivalries, cultural superiority, military prowess, and their god(s) reflected those priorities. People offered sacrifices hoping to escape the ire of a god that might be in a bad mood. Their version of god was simply one of luck and happenstance, which left everyone in a constant state of insecurity.

Some of the gods of the Greco-Roman world were Zeus the sky god, and being male he was naturally the supreme god. There was Athena, the goddess of war and justice, and Eros the god of sex and love. The idea of multiple deities was not restricted to the Greco-Roman world; the Hindus had their gods too. One was Indra the god of law and justice, another Mitra, god of friendship and contractual responsibilities, and Varuna, god of sky and water. In some parts of Africa, the spirit-gods were Nyama as the source of energy. The Earth was a god, being the incarnation of spirit, and Fire a god as the source of power. People in the Middle East viewed their gods as a royal aristocracy with themselves being the peasant class under them.

There was one common thread that ran through all of the created gods of antiquity, as different as they were, and that was their utilitarian aspect. Most all of them were "value-added gods" in the sense they were believed to be providers of tangible benefits to the people. Many of those gods were easily offended by humans and they were often in conflict with each other.

Others were actually indifferent to routine day-to-day human activity, and they did not inspire or require morality. Their temperamental dispositions needed to be continuously placated in some manner.

One of the downsides of cultivating a world view based on those ideas about a deity is the belief that if the gods cannot get along, why should we? Contrast that with the God of Abraham, Isaac, and Jacob, who dealt with three people differently, but whose intent behind the interactions with the three was the pursuit of love. Some would argue that the God of the Hebrew Scriptures was an angry judge, and the Commandments were given to keep order in the metaphorical court in which we live. If that has been your understanding, I would ask you to remember this: The judges on reality shows such as *America's Got Talent* are not there to speak to how bad the contestants are—they want someone to win. God the judge wants those who belong to him to win too. Our problem is our reluctance to agree with God about what it actually means to win.

The first Commandment is clear that God was concerned with the well-being of the Israelite community as a whole. There was no special favoring of any one individual or subset over the other. God said "I am yours" to each of them and all of them. Unlike the voiceless warring gods of old, the God of the Bible has given us a clearly defined assignment, and that is to love one another. Yet human history reveals Christians doing just the opposite century after century, all while professing Christ. In modern America, the negative sociological impact that this metaphorical split personality has had on people of color is incalculable. Which one of many possible areas should we study to gauge the harmful after effects?

We could start with a book by Thomas Shapiro, whose very title alone should signal the complexities involved in identifying the negative effects of racism. I recommend Shapiro's *The Hidden Cost of Being African American: How Wealth Perpetuates Inequality*. This book looks at the many ways that belonging to a minority culture results in limited access to opportunities throughout every area of life. Every ethical system is formed around a concept of justice, but where the perception of racial inferiority is accepted as axiomatic, then injustice prevails. One of the roots of misunderstanding in black/white relationships is that many white people believe justice is blind and that it doesn't see color—while many black people believe justice is deaf and it doesn't hear the cries about the unequal treatment meted out to them. How do you hear the cries of the poor and marginalized, as whining or legitimate?

Be-ing While Black

What follows is an excerpt from a recent interview that I participated in for my friend Paul Louis Metzger's blog, that demonstrates the way that different perceptions concerning any one story or event can result in so much disagreement between well-intentioned people:

> PLM: Sometimes one hears the expression "Driving while black."
> What does that mean?
>
> JC: It means many things but for me it is ultimately rooted in one word, "Belonging." One of the first waves of justification for the killing of Trayvon Martin while walking in a Florida suburb was "he didn't belong there." Meaning the person that ultimately killed him was right to note his presence, and then follow him in order to see what he was up to. Perhaps it is due to the segregation laws of the past, or today's practice of self-segregating, but it is assumed that one type of person belongs in a certain place and others don't. Automobiles provide black people the ability to be in those places [where] they traditionally did not belong and with that comes extra scrutiny by the police. They often feel it is part of their duty to check them out and see why they are there in the first place. Then any minor traffic violation or infraction becomes the justification for finding out why things are "out of order." There are many who would say it should be perfectly understandable that police would give extra attention to someone they see in a neighborhood that she or he doesn't belong in.[6]

We will look at some of the natural consequences of that perception in another chapter.

Listen to this from a not-so-distant past. In a book titled *Black Indians*, William Katz records that just prior to the Civil War people were actually paid to patrol neighborhoods looking for runaway slaves in places they did not belong. He stated that, "Savage beatings awaited any African American man, woman, and child walking without a pass." I am sure a great many of you are of the opinion that things have changed and that using examples from so far back in our history are not relevant or helpful. But racism remains a constant even when the method and intensity changes. Listen to this personal anecdote from that same interview with Paul Metzger, and

6. Metzger, "Driving While Black," para. 6.

perhaps it will provide you with more understanding about how race is still a factor in everyday life. I said:

> I attended a pastor conference during the time that the Trayvon Martin case was in the news. My hotel was situated a few yards off a major highway. Down the road about one-half mile was a traffic light and if you were to turn right at the street you would soon be in a residential community. I love to run in the morning for exercise. That morning I made the decision that it was safer to run on the highway—dodging the semis, distracted drivers, and other hazards posed by early morning rush hour traffic—rather than run in a dimly lit, and presumably heavily armed neighborhood in Texas where I didn't belong. Belonging assumes one has the right to be where they want to be, and be with whom they please, and that is the essence of *belonging* in a free society. In the example above I did not feel that I belonged due to the signals being sent by the majority of people that I encountered from the hotel staff, to the people in the restaurants, right down to the conference attenders.[7]

The verb "be" basically means to live, and living implies a freedom to explore possibilities. The sense of be-ing comfortable was never an option for me because people sent multiple signals indicating I was too different to belong. When I share these types of experiences with my white friends, they typically find other explanations for what happened. They say things such as "you are imagining it," or "you are hypersensitive." Some will make excuses for the perpetrators even when they were not present to observe the behavior. Racism is real, and it is hurtful, and just because one group has not felt its sting does not mean it has been defeated. Unfortunately, when we reduce racism to improper speech, or the occasional overt discriminatory act, we lose sight of the fact that racism is first and foremost an attitude shared by many.

Seeing Color Everywhere

Throughout America's history, the belief in the existence of different races has led to each race receiving different treatment, and it continues on to this day. Race, as determined by skin color, could be an idea borrowed from a seventeenth-century Dutch philosopher named Benedict Spinoza. Mr.

---

7. Metzger, "Driving While Black," para. 7.

Spinoza stated, "Two substances having different attributes have nothing in common with one another."[8] To be clear, I am not attempting to superimpose any connotation on that quote—those are simply his words. Perhaps Mr. Spinoza was only echoing Aristotle's view on the relationship between the colors black and white. Aristotle believed the two colors to be on "opposites at the extreme ends of an ordered range of colors."[9]

That understanding may have been applied to the way the European colonizers viewed human beings, and so it seemed logical to them that people of "opposite" colors would not, and should not, have anything in common with each other. Mr. Spinoza anticipated that application by suggesting, "Those things which have nothing mutually in common with one another cannot through one another be mutually understood."[10] Many attribute their attitudes about perceived racial difference to natural instinct, cultural norms, and the most recent culprit, science. Let us look at how far off the path of common sense the latter can go.

Not long ago I became interested in the way people have used science to advance race theory. One article theorized that Negroes had a disease that was particular to them called Dysaethesia Aethiopica, which produced "Rascality," meaning someone prone to troublemaking. The symptoms of this "disease" were said to include, "Much mischief, which appears as if intentional, but is mostly owing to the stupidity of mind and insensibility of the nerves induced by the disease."[11] Since there was no known cure for that dreaded disease, more separation from the diseased population was deemed prudent. I note this for two reasons. The first being that is just funny, and I hope it hit you that way. Just so you know, much of the race science I read today sounds just as crazy—it has just not been discredited yet.

The second reason is to point out that we seem to be wedded to the idea that everything we need to know can be accessed scientifically. What is the goal of that enterprise? Is it to know, control, or manipulate? As we have just seen, science should not be what a scientist theorizes, speculates, or even demands that society accepts for the sake of progress. Science is more than a well-articulated set of theories, it is fact-based, and I do not believe there will ever be a provable scientific theory that will support racism.

8. Spinoza, *Ethics*, 4.

9. Kalderon, *Form without Matter*, 24.

10. Spinoza, *Ethics*, 4.

11 Dr. Cartwright, "Dysaethesia Aethiopica," para. 6, line 1.

Who Are You, Who Are We?

Several years ago, Richard Dawkins theorized about something he called the selfish gene. A Wikipedia article explained, "From the gene-centered view, it follows that the more two individuals are genetically related, the more sense (at the level of the genes) it makes for them to behave selflessly with each other."[12] Let us hone in on this "gene-centered" view. For the majority of my life I held a gene-centered view related to what made us human. I believed that our genes determined our characteristics, and also which of those traits were passed on. I believed that genes determined whether or not I liked steak, was left-handed, able to sing, or preferred the mountains to the beach. I believed that genes were the direct cause for just about every characteristic that made me who I was. Most people who believed that genes were the determinate cause of our makeup also accepted that a version of survival of the fittest occurred among our genes. In other words, only the strongest and best genes advanced by dominating other genes—just as supposedly happens between people.

Biologist Denis Noble discovered that genes do not always function in that way. There are times when they actually cooperate with each other in groups or networks. He characterized it this way in his book *The Music of Life*: "We sometimes say things like, 'a gene does such and such' but that sort of statement tends to be misleading. A gene will do one thing in one set of circumstances and another if the circumstances change."[13] In America, the majority culture's view of race is much like the view many have about genes, and that is that race (genes) determines everything! It should encourage us to learn that genes act differently at times—and that genes cooperate with different genes for the good of the whole. Genes do not always view other genes as outsiders. Genes seem to be able to find a way to coexist out of physiological necessity to perform their intended function. Perhaps if we were to take a lesson from our genes, we could coexist in a similar fashion.

Better Together

It is sad that at this late stage many, including Christians, hold very strong opinions about miscegenation—meaning intimate "race-mixing." The looks of disapproval that my (white) wife and I receive in churches would

12. Wikipedia, "The Selfish Gene," line 1.

13. Noble, *Music of Life*, 104–5.

astonish you. Not in 2019, you say? What follows is a recent example of that, and it might help you change your mind. In 2017 an English Prince and an American actress announced their engagement. That news set the traditional and social media abuzz. I perused comments made on Facebook, as well as various print articles, and here are some paraphrased examples of the anger voiced about their engagement. The comments had one thing in common—the people making them all viewed race much like I had genetics—it determined everything!

One person was outraged that someone would compare the Prince's brother's wife, the white Duchess Kate, to a black American low-level actress. In another comment, someone said that the Duchess was a white Anglo-Saxon, whereas Meghan Markle was half black. To this person that meant they had nothing in common. One other person said that English royalty had always married "their own kind," presumably upper-class aristocrats. This person was amazed at the possibility that the royal family would break with tradition and allow the royal bloodline to be tainted by a mixed-race woman. Let's contrast the European perspective we just listened to with the African way. "If someone from another village marries one from another village, both villages become family."[14]

Racializing love exposes the degree to which intolerance is normalized in our society because marriage is the ultimate sign of belonging. Racialized determinism not only bolsters the idea of white superiority—it strengthens the concept of brown and black inferiority. Granted the two are different sides of the same coin, but the negative effects they produce are extremely harmful, regardless of which side of the coin is visible.

Belonging is what unifies all of creation and a refusal to extend a hand is a misuse of the gospel message. It is hard for me to relate to people holding the view that some people are more loved by God than others. Many not only advance that doctrine, but they find comfort in it. A misunderstanding of the meaning of the word *chosen* is at the root of this thinking. I hope this last illustration will communicate my understanding of what it means to be chosen by God. The idea for this illustration comes from a recent meme. One frame at the top of the meme depicted Adolf Hitler saluting the Nazi troops with a caption that read, "We are the master race."[15] Next to it was a frame with Israel's Prime Minister in a posture similar to Hitler's, but he was waving to a crowd of admirers—and the caption read, "We are the

14. Doumbia, *Way of the Elders*, 107.
15. Hitler Meme.

chosen people."[16] Directly beneath the two frames was a third about the size of the other two combined that asked, "What's the difference?"[17]

Actually, there is a major difference between the Jewish and German understanding of the word *chosen*. The German version of *chosen* was rooted in nationalism—and used to prove that they were naturally selected to be the "master race," meaning superior. However, religious Jews did not understand the word *chosen* to mean that they were a superior race, only that they were being selected by God for a specific purpose. That purpose is found in the idea of *tikkun olam*, which means to repair the world for the benefit of all. Christians advance that ideal through obeying Jesus' command to love every people-group in existence, meaning our neighbors and our enemies. Take a few minutes to create a mental picture of your neighbors, and then draw one of your enemies. Now, ask yourself what it is that you could do to transform the people that you perceive to be an enemy into a neighbor.

16. Hitler Meme.
17. Hitler Meme.

3

Perspectives

You Shall Not Make for Yourself an Idol (Exod 20:4–6).

WHERE DO THE MORAL codes that you live by originate? Many people say that they are simply the sum total of well-reasoned choices on the part of every individual. Others believe we align our behavior to correspond with the morality that our culture, ethnic group, or political party holds as correct. There are still others within the scientific community who speculate that neither reason, nor any external influence, has anything to do with how a person arrives at which moral codes to follow. Their assumptions are that since human beings are little more than an amalgam of genes, bacteria, neurons, and tissue, behaviors are shaped unconsciously by the environment. Each of those perspectives is quite different, are they not? Which of these perspectives would you perceive to be the most accurate? Perceptions of morality are derived from whatever the perspective is that the person brings with them.

Perspectives are the preexisting beliefs that are embedded in our minds long before we encounter the need to apply them. Roman Emperor Marcus Aurelius expressed much the same idea when he said, "If anyone can refute me—show me I'm making a mistake or looking at things from the wrong perspective—I'll gladly change. It's the truth I'm after, and the truth never harmed anyone. What harms us is to persist in self-deceit and ignorance."[1] The way he looked at something, perception, came "from" his

1. Goodreads.com, "Marcus Aurelius," para. 1.

perspective. For our conversation about morality, perspectives precede perception. Over time, we learn to rely on those preexisting ideas, perspectives, to make judgments about what is moral—irrespective of how harmful the ethics produced by them may be to others. But is there more? Should there be more?

Rabbi Abraham Heschel once said, "To rely on our faith would be idol-worship. We have only the right to rely on God."[2] When I first ran across this quote it troubled me to a certain degree. I had spent the majority of my adult life encouraging people to develop enough faith to fully trust God in every area of their lives—now someone I respect implies that I could have been leading them into a form of idol worship. That just did not sit right with me, for many reasons. It required several passes at this quote before I realized that my unease was due to the fact that I might have been missing the point. My role in the church caused me to focus on the two words, *faith* and *God*, so intently that I overlooked one keyword—*rely*. The Oxford Dictionary defines the word *rely* as to "Depend on with full trust or confidence."[3] So, when it comes to identifying the best source for morals, who or what should we place our full trust and confidence in? God! The ultimate test of a moral code is whether or not it molds people's character in such a way that they seek justice for, and humane treatment of, others. Would you not agree history proves we have had a hard time doing both things at the same time?

The majority of people from Western cultures have relied on various versions of God as their source of morality for centuries. However, in 2017 best-selling author Dan Brown put forward the idea that a "collective consciousness" could soon become a replacement for God! He made this remark while promoting the book *Origin* that he said was inspired by the question, "Will God survive science?"[4] The author went on to say, "We will start to find our spiritual experiences through our interconnections with each other—forecasting the emergence of some form of global consciousness that we perceive and that becomes our divine."[5] Mr. Brown followed that idea with this comment, "Our need for that exterior god, that sits up there and judges us . . . will diminish and eventually disappear."[6] Even if

2. Merkle, *Approaching God,* 75.

3. Lexico.com, "Rely," line 1.

4 Busvine, "Collective Consciousness to Replace God," para. 3.

5. Busvine, "Collective Consciousness to Replace God," para. 13.

6. Busvine, "Collective Consciousness to Replace God," para. 14.

his speculations are accurate, is 2017 the first time in human history that a large number of people have made the decision to try and replace God? Not really! Let us consider for a moment what the circumstances were like in the Israelite community at the time the Ten Words were received.

Replacing God

When Moses left the Israelites for Mount Sinai to receive the Ten Words, they became increasingly nervous by his prolonged absence. Remember, Moses had spent forty days away from them, and it is reasonable to believe the people had moved beyond nervousness to "freaking out." One constant throughout all of history is that since people are unable to foresee the future, they are prone to believe that there is no God out there to control it. Uncertainty can cause people to create a god of their own. They create something they can see to replace the God they cannot see. People can trust in a host of visible and practical "gods," such as socioeconomic status, race, and the material things that bring them a sense of security. Ironically, a few will put their trust in material things, even if they have to go into debt to pay for them. In some ways, that is what the Israelites did when they commissioned Aaron to melt their gold earrings down to make a golden idol. The idol he made for them was a calf, but it could have been a beachfront house in Manhattan Beach, California, a vintage 51 P-bass guitar, or a Ferrari. I just revealed some of my "golden calves," did I not?

Several years ago, during rock and roll's infancy, a song was popular by a vocal group named the Coasters. The lyrics to that song told the story of a kid who had purchased an idol with a golden head. The song's premise was in some ways a repeat of the biblical story about the Israelites and their golden calf. In this song, the singer placed this inanimate idol on a shelf above his bed, and suddenly a bolt of lightning brought the statue to life. When the idol began to speak, he listened because it was telling him things that he wanted to hear. The song goes on to chronicle the conversation that ensued between the idol and the singer. As time passed the idol made it clear that it was in the singer's corner. Notice that in the song there required some type of activation to occur for the idol to become real. The same holds true for the idols we create because a trigger must occur in us too. That trigger is typically molded from our desire to have our lives go as we planned. When we perceive our desires are being fulfilled, we attribute whatever is making us happy at that moment to the activities of the idols we created.

Trusting God

One afternoon during a conversation with an attorney friend named Michael Lawrence I casually made a comment that a lawyer had a moral duty to be ethical. He responded by saying morals and ethics were interchangeable concepts and off we went on to a lengthy and unplanned philosophical debate. I decided to use an illustration from the sports world to buttress my argument, and that was the concept of fairness. I said that fairness was not a moral issue, but a matter of ethics. In our culture, the concepts of ethics and fairness are similar in that they are both rules for how to play a game. Whether it is the game of life or some form of human competition, rules do matter. For this reason, a moral code is necessary to drive ethics because human beings are notorious for changing the rules of any game they devise. It should then follow that if morals are to exist at all, then they must originate from a source independent of any human rules committee that can alter what is right or wrong.

Morality addresses what is right and what is wrong. While ethics address which behaviors are good and just. Morality and the ethics that are derived from them are also about more than human behavior. Theologian James McClendon said, "So ethics, and the morality that ethics is about, lay at the threshold of theology."[8] Yes, they are different in some sense, and yes they are both necessary, and they both point to God.

Many people eschew the idea that objective morals, as determined by a living God, actually exist. They would much prefer that morals could have been developed biologically. During one of my small group meetings a spirited discussion was launched about whether or not people were born knowing right from wrong. The consensus within this group of loving, very smart, and well-educated professional people was that human beings do possess some type of morality gene known as the "gut feeling." My friends believe that people are born knowing what the right thing to do is, but for some unknown reason a few just choose to do the wrong thing. There is even a scientific theory that purports to prove that human beings do not need an external moral code to live ethically. Donald W. Pfaff writes in *The Altruistic Brain,* "After centuries of debate over whether humanity is fundamentally flawed (as blamed on Eve) or particularly benevolent (as proposed by Philosopher David Hume), neuroscience is ready to provide the answer:

8. McClendon, *Ethics,* 42.

we are in fact good."[9] He went on to say, "That is, we are instinctively good and the idea is now ready for prime time."[10]

It may massage our egos to think that we have evolved to the point that human intuition, in combination with natural law, can guide us in matters of morality. But history indicates that when human beings follow their natural inclinations, fairness rarely follows. When the histories of people from diverse backgrounds lead to conflicting conclusions, it becomes impossible to establish a moral code that is satisfactory to all. That is why it is clear to me that we can never arrive at an agreement about what is fair without some type of impartial and external code for determining ethics. Then what should be used for deciding how we should all live? Mr. Pfaff may believe neuroscience has located the key for unlocking human morality—but I am not convinced that morality is actually within the purview of science.

Remember, it was not that long ago that scientists made claims that women were essentially inferior to men. That Africans were subhuman, and Native Americans were not physiologically strong enough to consume alcohol. Perhaps we should not just simply accept that science has primacy over religion as it relates to human behavior. If morals exist, and if they did originate with God, we should probably try harder to trust him rather than seeking alternative explanations for them.

Idols with Golden Heads

Adolf Hitler is the poster child for immorality in our society. One of his perspectives that was not discredited was that the perfect human being would have blond hair with blue eyes. Google the American standard for beauty, and you will find some that allude to something beautiful as having qualities that please the senses, especially the sight. However, it is this definition found in the Oxford Dictionary that is most relevant: "he arrived with a blonde beauty on his arm."[11] How many times have you heard someone say "blond-haired blue-eyed beauty" when describing the American ideal? No, I am not equating America's racial attitudes with Hitler's. And I am not drawing a moral equivalence between the two. However, if we are honest, some of his beliefs about the innate worth of a human being are

9. Pfaff, *The Altruistic Brain*, 10.
10. Pfaff, *The Altruistic Brain*, 10.
11. Oxforddictionaries.com, "Beauty," section 2, line 1.

alive and well in today's America. Today may be the right time to redevelop the perspective that everyone created by God is good, as stated in Genesis. I think were we to do so, our perception of what is beautiful, and what is not, would change dramatically.

Let me restate that I am not drawing a moral equivalence between German race theory of old and American race theory, but it is fair to point out similarities. Consider some of the "race science" that was popular at the time of Hitler's ascent to power. A German Darwinian biologist hypothesized, "Some races in Africa and Asia have no concept of marriage or the family; like apes, they live in herds, climb trees and eat fruit."[12] I would imagine that many of you who are white are appalled by such a statement, and cannot imagine that those ideas were accepted as legitimate science. But they were.

What would you think if a scientist were to write an article in your hometown newspaper stating that every black male between eighteen and thirty-five wearing their pants low is a sure sign that they have a low IQ and are prone to violence? Additionally, they must be supervised by police in order to curb their natural inclination towards criminal behavior. Hitler's racial perspectives were not original. His ideology was shaped years before he had any power to act on them. For example, before Hitler came to power, the German evolutionary scientist Ernst Haeckel wrote, "The Caucasian, or Mediterranean man (*Homo Mediterraneus*), has from time immemorial been placed at the head of all the races of men, as the most highly developed and perfect."[13]

Why are there so many that still hold that view in 2019? It is because these types of perspectives have been planted into our cultural understanding through myth, books, television, film, and other forms of media. Consider this recent British television offering for an example. The name of the series was *The Last Kingdom* and it was shot in 2017. The two male leads were brothers. One brother, blond-haired Erik, was portrayed as a good-hearted heroic figure. The second brother Siegfried was dark-haired and portrayed as being cruel, shady, and vicious. Even the horses used in the series were selected to align with the standard assumption that lighter is good and darker is bad. The horse that the good king rode, and the horse the heroic lead Uhtred rode, were both white.

12. Bergman, *The Darwin Effect*, 108.
13. Haeckel, *The History of Creation*, 429.

Contrast that with the black horses that the bad King Aethlewold and his conniving sidekick Aldhelm rode. The imagery was clear and pointed. The choices made by the producers were selected to fit the preestablished understanding of the intended audience. The dark/bad, versus light/good, juxtaposition is indelibly etched into the psyche of our country. The pride that color-based racial groups engender can almost reach the level of idol status and as idolatry, it is much more prevalent than many would care to admit.

I'm Bad and They Knew It

I lived in Sherman Oaks, California at a time when computerized banking did not exist. Before moving to Southern California, I had lived in a beach town named Santa Cruz in the northern part of the state. Some months prior to moving south I had turned in a lost checkbook notification to the Bank of America. In response, they placed a hold on a series of checks that were adjacent to the numbers that were lost. One of the safeguards that the bank had in place to protect the account holders was something called a signature card. That was a card kept at the branch that contained some personal information that only the actual customer should know, with a copy of their signature for comparison. One day I needed a small amount of cash but did not have my checkbook with me. I decided to go to my branch and ask for what was called a "counter check." That was a blank check that a teller would write in the customer's account information, making it as legitimate as a preprinted check. Using a counter check to withdraw money was something that I had done several times in the past. To this point, there had never been a problem with the process—but that was about to change.

The information on my signature card included my birth date, my social security number, my mother's maiden name (which was Highshaw), her place of birth (which was Smackover, Arkansas), plus a couple of more items that were equally unusual. I entered the bank, asked for a counter check, then waited for the teller to verify my information and return. She was gone for an inordinate amount of time, but I did not become particularly concerned until she returned with a supervisor. The supervisor informed me that there was a problem because there was a lost check hold from the Santa Cruz branch. I explained that I was aware of the hold, but that I had received a counter check previously without a problem. Additionally, I had lived in Sherman Oaks for some time, and I had cashed counter checks at this very branch without difficulty. We had a lengthy discussion during which she reiterated over and over that the process was for my protection. I responded that I understood, but the signature card was created by me for just this type of scenario, and to please consider how unusual the names on it were.

What I was not aware of at the time was that the teller had identified me as a person suspected in a string of armed robberies and called the police. It is important for you to understand that the picture on the wanted poster looked nothing like me except for that fact both of our skins were darker than hers. I had very long hair, and his hair was short. I was thin, and he was stocky. His listed height was 5' 8," and I was 6' 0." I asked to speak to their "higher up" not knowing they were trying to keep me there until the police could arrive. They did not succeed. Frustrated, I made my way back to my car.

Racing through my mind was the thought of having to drive all the way into Hollywood to get some cash from my management. I sat there for a few minutes to allow my anger to subside and decided to listen to a song on the radio. The song ended, and just as I was about to start my car, the door opened—*boom!*—I was pulled out of the car and thrown to the ground by a police officer. Within seconds I was face down on the loose gravel with a foot in my back, while another officer was grabbing and twisting my other arm in order to handcuff me. When I was able to look up, I saw several guns pointed directly at me as one officer quipped, "You're lucky you didn't start that car or we would have opened fire."

Apparently, the entire time I was listening to the song on the radio, there had been an officer on a bullhorn instructing me to get out of the car. I did not comply with the officer's order because the volume of my car's stereo made his overtures inaudible. Because of that, I wound up handcuffed on the ground with my face bloodied. One was pulling on my hair thinking it was a wig, while another shouted racial epithets at me. Once I was in the back seat of a patrol car, an officer sat next to me asking ridiculous questions not at all related to bank robbery. When I did not respond in a manner he liked, he poked me in the rib with his nightstick extremely hard. After what seemed like an eternity, a higher ranking, and much calmer, officer approached and asked me some sensible questions. I told him my story, and his response upon hearing Smackover, Arkansas was to shake his head and say, "You're kidding?"

That officer went back into the bank and a few minutes later he came out. He then had the other officers remove the cuffs and apologized. He informed me that he thought the teller was way out of line since the description of the actual suspect was not even close to a physical match to mine. The teller made a perceptual error based upon an almost universally accepted white perspective that people of African descent are more hardwired to commit crimes than other races. In our culture, perceptions are relative to their objects. One of the by-products of the belief in biological racial difference is the belief that people within their own group are even more moral than those belonging to that other group. They are convinced that is accurate while overlooking the fact that all of humanity shares the same history of bad acts.

Perspective Precedes Perception

One thing to remember as we end this chapter is that our perspectives really do matter. Our perspectives, meaning the preexisting understandings we hold about any given subject, will fuel what it is we believe to be reasonable. For example, I played the bass line on Funkadelic's hit "Comin' Round the Mountain." I read a reviewer who raved about the bass line because he understood it to have been played by the more famous Bootsy Collins. He perceived the bass line to be great because his preexisting understanding was that Bootsy was a great musician. This reviewer judged my playing through the lens of his preexisting admiration for Bootsy's overall body of work. That resulted in my playing on that record being perceived as better than it might have been had the reviewer known it was me playing and not Bootsy. In a similar way, perspectives influence the way we perceive the world and the people around us because they contextualize our perception.

If we hold on to the perspective, i.e., preexisting understanding, that racial groups are essentially different from each other based on external appearance alone, we will act accordingly. That means that as with the record reviewer, we will see value where it may or may not exist, and possibly little value where it does exist, simply because of the perspectives that we had going in. If you want to develop the skill to see the others accurately, work hard to rearrange what it is you believed about them from the start—those beliefs are your perspectives, and they can change.

4

Naming

You Shall Not Take the Name
of the Lord Your God in Vain (Exod 20:7).

IN 1962 A YOUNG singer-songwriter named Robert Zimmerman arrived in New York in search of fortune and fame. This was the era when being "cool" was what the average young person aspired to in America. Cool altered the mode of dress and speech by which those immersed in Western popular culture expressed themselves. Blogger Alexander Kahn cited Joel Dinerstein defining cool as "synonymous with authenticity, independence, integrity, and nonconformity; to be cool meant you carried personal authority through a stylish mask of stoicism."[1] Jazz trumpeter Miles Davis was cool, and his type of cool was suave, sophisticated, and exploratory. James Dean was cool too, but his version was that of a rebel and contrarian who was searching for meaning in a world of meaninglessness. The Beat generation of the 1950s, with its existentialist emphasis on the right to self-determination, provided the foundation for cool.

A Wikipedia article states that "Central elements of Beat culture are (were) rejection of standard narrative values, spiritual quest, exploration of American and Eastern religions, rejection of materialism, explicit portrayals of the human condition, experimentation with psychedelic drugs, and sexual liberation and exploration."[2] Cool challenged the majority of

1. Kahn, "The Land of the Free," line 14.
2. Wikipedia, "Beat Generation," line 2.

35

late 1950s cultural assumptions by being indifferent to them. Being cool was an attempt to protest against what was viewed as a staid, uptight, and restrictive society—and not with words alone, but by a commitment to a countercultural lifestyle.

That was the world in which a young Bob Zimmerman sought to make his mark, and in that world a name like Zimmerman would have probably been more of a hindrance than a help. When the time came that this very talented musician procured a recording contract, he went from being known as "uncool" Bob Zimmerman, to the very cool and also legal Bob Dylan. He changed his name and with that came a complete change of direction for his life. White Americans not only approved of his decision, they celebrated it, and then embraced him as one of their brightest stars and the voice of a generation. Listen to the words of the English poet William Shakespeare, "What's in a name? That which we call a rose, By any other name would smell as sweet."[3]

One might conclude from Mr. Shakespeare's sonnet that names are not that important and they are interchangeable. That did not prove to be true for another individual who was choosing to make a similar decision around the same time. This man, whose given name was Cassius Marcellus Clay, would in a short while become an American cultural icon in his own right. Following his winning the world's heavyweight boxing title, a young Cassius converted to the Nation of Islam. He decided that he no longer wanted a name given to his forebears by their slave masters. Many white people at the time viewed the Muslim religion to be more African in nature than their Eurocentric version of Christianity. His embrace of an "exotic" faith, combined with the rejection of his anglicized name, infuriated white America, and a major controversy erupted.

Black America applauded Muhammad Ali for standing up for his personhood, but white America perceived his stance as a disruption to the proper order they had worked so hard to establish. On February 6, 1967 Cassius Clay, who had recently changed his name to Muhammad Ali, fought a man named Ernie Terrell for the heavyweight boxing championship of the world. Many whites viewed the fight to be a battle between the wholesomeness of the American way of life versus the radicalism of a strange religion. A significant number of whites also hated Ali for opposing a war in Vietnam that was becoming increasingly unpopular. To give his

---

3. Wikipedia, "A rose by any other name," line 1.

position on the war more clarity, Mr. Ali stated that no Vietnamese had ever named him "nigger" and he did not hold any animus towards them.

Calling Someone out They Name

To use the vernacular of the day, "calling someone out they name" had to do with a person being disrespected by another because that person addressed them in a manner of their choosing rather than yours. One example is that some people used to call an adult black male "boy," even when the person knew both his name and his age. An example of the after-effect of calling someone "out they name" can be seen in what occurred one February night in a boxing ring in Houston. The fight between Muhammad Ali and Ernie Terrell became an event of major cultural importance. The location of the fight testified to the fact that this was an event that transcended sports. The fight was staged at the Houston Astrodome, considered to be one of the architectural wonders of the time because it was the world's first multipurpose, domed sports stadium.

A part of the prefight build-up revolved around boxer Ernie Terrell calling the champion Muhammad Ali out his name. Mr. Terrell refused to refer to Mr. Ali by his chosen name and he continually used Muhammad Ali's "slave name," Cassius Clay, instead. That refusal incensed Ali, but it garnered Mr. Terrell an enormous amount of support in the white community and on fight night many hoped he would put Mr. Ali in his "place."

In America, professional sports are more of a market-driven entertainment enterprise than a platform for athletes to simply compete for the sake of competition. Like many other businesses, success depends on sales, and sales often times require promotion or other forms of marketing. Muhammad Ali was not only a superb athlete—he was also an adroit marketer. In order to promote himself he often created narratives that portrayed him as a villain. He implanted certain themes in the public mind, such as him having a big mouth, being arrogant about his skill set, and in this instance, possibly being unpatriotic. Here is my transcription of a pre-fight exchange. Muhammad Ali speaks first:

> "Why don't you call me my name, man?" Ernie Terrell said, "Well, what's your name? You told me it was Cassius Clay." Ali responded, "I never told you my name is Cassius Clay. My name is Muhammad Ali and you will announce it right there in the center of that

ring after the fight, if you don't do it now. You are acting just like an old 'Uncle Tom,' another Floyd Patterson. I'm gonna punish you!"[4]

I watched a video replay of the actual fight and Mr. Ali was clearly agitated from the opening bell. True to his word, Muhammad Ali punished Ernie Terrell by completely dominating him for fifteen brutal rounds. During every round an exasperated Ali would ask his bemused and befuddled opponent, "What's my name?" and then he would continue to pummel him mercilessly. Many boxing experts believed that Mr. Ali carried the outmatched Ernie Terrell for the entire fifteen rounds just to punish him for his unwillingness to call him Muhammad Ali. In fact, some sports writers commenting on the fight said that Mr. Ali lost stature because of the treatment he doled out. They perceived it to be harsh to the point of vindictive. If it was vindictive, it could be evidence of the high value many, including God, place on being addressed properly. Mr. Dylan had changed his name for commercial reasons, whereas Muhammad Ali changed his for religious and political reasons, and those changes were received quite differently by 1960s white America:

> You find that there are three names by which a person is called,
> one which his father and mother call him,
> and one which people call him,
> and one which he earns for himself,
> best of all is the one he earns for himself.[5]

In popular music there are many song titles that ask questions either of the singer or the listener. Ironically, some of those titles are questions that many people have asked about God. Songs like, "Who Are You?" by The Who, "How Will I Know?" by Whitney Houston, and "What's Love Got to Do with It?" by Tina Turner come to mind. Sadly, the question asked by the last title could be asked of Christians who seek blessing from God but are reluctant to see themselves blessing others, such as marginalized people. That said, it is a song by southern rockers Lynyrd Skynyrd titled, "What's Your Name?" that is relevant to our discussion. That is because at one point in Moses' life he was asked by the ruler of Egypt the very same question about his God: "What is his name?"

---

4. Youtube.com, "Muhammad Ali vs. Ernie Terrell."
5. Oz and Salzberger, *jews and words,* 14.

Author Thomas Cahill relates a similar question being asked by the Israelites themselves in his book *The Gift of The Jews*. The backstory is that God had told Moses to deliver a message about freedom to a group of people that had been slaves all of their lives, and Moses knew that they would doubt him. Mr. Cahill writes, "Moshe (Moses) imagines confronting the Children of Israel with, 'the God of your fathers has sent me,' only to receive the skeptical response: 'They will say to me: 'What is his name?'"[6] The only answer that they would receive was not a very satisfying one, the almost non-responsive "YHWH!" Simply put, this was an unpronounceable set of letters to introduce the unidentifiable one. Rabbi Sacks gives more insight into this important concept when he describes what came out of Moses' mouth as, "the four letter name we may not pronounce, known generally as Hashem—'The Name.'"[7]

Name above All Names

If you were to Google the words "true name" you would find an article that says, "A true name is the name of a thing or being that expresses, or is somehow identical with, its true nature."[8] A theme that runs through many fantasy books is that if you find someone's true name, you can get unlimited power over them, or take their power from them. That characterization of the power in a name is of course fantasy, but as it is with many myths, there is a kernel of truth mixed in. Names as identifiers have power, and they have far more power than most admit.

The Hebrew people believed that names were important because they not only distinguished one person from another—they were often used to describe a person's attributes. A name was how you came to know someone. Moses' name was also descriptive of the facts surrounding his early childhood. The story goes that as a toddler he was pulled out of the water by an Egyptian princess and she used a word meaning "drawn out" to name him. There are some scholars who believe the Hebrew verb *Moshe* was derived from even older Egyptian roots, with one being the verb "*ms/msi* (to give birth)."[9] If true, then it is plausible that Moses' Egyptian name identi-

6. Cahill, *The Gift of the Jews,* 114.
7. Sacks, *Covenant & Conversation,* 38.
8. Wikipedia, "True Name," line 3.
9. Bibleodessey.org, "Was Moses' name Egyptian?" para. 5, line 2.

fied him as a person, Moshe, born of water—and his Hebrew name Moses spoke of his destiny as the deliverer. That is amazing.

This section got its title from a Christian worship song that Julaine and I have sung over and over. It said God's name is *above all*, meaning different from every other name, and more important than every other name. Let that settle in a bit and then consider why names were important to many religious and nonreligious Jews. "In Jewish thought, a name is not merely an arbitrary designation, a random combination of sounds. The name conveys the nature and essence of the thing named. It represents the history and reputation of the being named."[10] Moses was not asking God, "What are your characteristics?" but "How will I know you?" The prayer named the *Shema* opens by asking the hearer to think about the name of God. Because it focuses on God's name, it is considered by many to be the most essential prayer in all of Judaism, and it is recited many times during the day. Rabbi Zimmerman emphasizes the degree of sacredness of *Shema* by saying, "These are the most important words a Jew can know because they speak of God's singularity and uniqueness."[11] The prayer's opening stanza says, "Hear O Israel the Lord is our God, The Lord is one."[12] Notice that it does not begin with a law or a principle, but an encouragement to hear, meaning to listen in order to fully grasp the meaning.

The *Shema* goes on to say that God is *one*! Could the emphasis on the word *one* be a Trinitarian reference? Possibly, but it could also be a warning not to invent names or labels for God like the surrounding cultures were in the habit of doing, because to the Jew and Christian alike, there really is only one. That means that all of the other deities people have worshiped would be fraudulent and unworthy of that particular name. Referring to God as something other than his chosen and preferred name is a form of abuse, if we define abuse as a misuse of something. Attributing something to his name that is inconsistent with what we know of his character is also a form of abuse. What follows is an extremely egregious example of a couple of committed Christians that misused the name of God in an unfathomable way.

10. Jewfaq.org, "The Name of G–d," line 1.

11. Dickson, *Gospel of Moses,* 29.

12. Deut 6:4, NIV.

Misusing the Name

The television program *Crime Watch Daily* produced a segment about a love triangle gone horribly wrong. A Christian woman named Sabrina Limon, who was married, conspired with a Christian man named Jonathan Hearn to kill her husband. The police had listened to phone exchanges between the couple after the murder and heard Sabrina allude to a spiritual element of their crime by saying, "There is a purpose for all of the things God has shown us."[13] The devout Christian triggerman replies, "Yes, yes there is Sabrina!"[14] During another wiretapped phone call Jonathan prayed, "God help us, Please God help us to be wise."[15] The wisdom he was seeking was for Sabrina to choose the right words when speaking to the police in order to avoid arrest. Sabrina's distorted view of God's plan for her life resulted in this prayer, "God, this is, this is what you want, you really want me to be with him."[16] The "him" in this prayer is the man that ambushed the father of her children and shot him dead! How could two regular church attenders feel no compunction about attaching God's name to their own twisted selfish desires as though their desires were part of a spiritual plan? In one frame they actually assured each other that their relationship was a "God thing"![17] Perhaps that illustrates why the only safeguard against substituting our own plan for God's is to take seriously the words in the Lord's Prayer where it says, "Your [God's] will be done."

The Name Game

I once lived in the Washington DC area. My home was actually located in Burtonsville, Maryland, but the nation's capital was a short distance as the crow flies. At that time there was a fierce debate swirling around the name of the local pro football team, the Washington Redskins. Indigenous people strongly objected to the name, while a considerable number of white people believed the controversy was much ado about nothing. I believe that the white indifference stemmed from a misunderstanding about why so many Native people were upset in the first place. We know that race plays a huge

13. Youtube.com, "Open Marriage."
14. Youtube.com, "Open Marriage."
15. Youtube.com, "Open Marriage."
16. Youtube.com, "Open Marriage."
17. Youtube.com, "Open Marriage."

role in most things American. Racial groups are identified by skin color, and so it is understandable that some would assume the name "Redskin" was just an innocent descriptor for a racial group. They would argue that the name is simply an accurate description of a physical characteristic, and that Native people should take pride in the name because after all that is who they are.

But what if the name "Redskins" elicited strong emotions from Native people for an entirely different reason than racial identity? Consider what a Native man named Dallas Goldtooth posted on the *Indian Country Today* website: "It was only five generations ago that a white man could get money for one of my grandfather's scalps. At this time . . . it was 'Redskin' that was used to describe us."[18] There is an image on the left of Mr. Goldtooth's article that depicts a newspaper clipping from an 1863 advertisement that said, "The State reward for dead Indians has been increased to $200 for every red-skin sent to Purgatory."[19] It appears that a short while later scalp hunting was renamed Indian fighting to legitimize the "savage" treatment the Europeans inflicted upon Native tribes.

When Native people refused to peacefully capitulate to demands to turn over their land and food to the new arrivals, Roxanne Dunbar-Ortiz writes, "As an incentive to recruit fighters, Colonial authorities introduced a program of scalp hunting that became a permanent and long lasting element of settler warfare against indigenous nations."[20] Another tool in the war chest utilized against Native people was to "call them out they name" in a similar fashion to what Mr. Terrell had done to Muhammad Ali, thereby devaluing and depersonalizing them.

What's My Name? I'm Not Sure

Roxanne Dunbar-Ortiz writes, "Native peoples were colonized and deposed of their territories as distinct peoples,"[21] which included being renamed. Ms. Dunbar-Ortiz cites some examples of the preferred Native names for their communities, and contrasts them with the "assigned" names such as "Dine (Navajo); Huade-Nosaunee (Iroquois); Tsalagi (Cherokee)."[22] A

18. Goldtooth, "Dakota Man," line 1.
19. Goldtooth, "Dakota Man," photo.
20. Dunbar-Ortiz, *An Indigenous People's History,* 64.
21. Dunbar-Ortiz, *An Indigenous People's History,* xiii.
22. Dunbar-Ortiz, *An Indigenous People's History,* xiii.

Native friend named Elmer gave me some insight into the how and why this renaming happened. He said that the name that his tribe is known by today was actually a word that was used for them by their enemies. The Europeans called his tribe by the name used by an enemy as a means of belittling them. Notice that the renaming of Native tribes is also a devaluing of them because they were forced to relinquish their historical identities. They no longer had the right to be themselves—they had to be who a group of people they had never met said they were. One of the more sobering aspects of the Native experience in the United States is similar to that of African people. The majority culture misused names and labels to define these darker-skinned people according to their prejudices, and it continues on to this present day.

One of the interesting narratives about the European colonization of the Americas is that it was achieved by the hard work of intact pure white nuclear families riding in wagon trains as they braved the "new" frontiers. Actually, as John Henrik Clarke wrote, "Comparatively few white women were brought to the New World during the first hundred years. Many families of the New World originated between white slave master and African women."[23] Additionally, historian Jacqueline Jones said of the longevity of the marriages in early Virginia, "when mortality rates were high—almost three quarters of immigrant men died before age fifty—and marriages were short, an average of seven years."[24] If survival depended on families producing offspring to assist in the difficult challenge of growing food, as well as establishing communities for mutual security, what would you imagine the most prudent method would be to achieve those goals? I would assume that young women and men of every skin hue would do what young people of every preceding and succeeding generation have done: engage in sexual relations.

If my assumption is accurate—and history appears to suggest that it is—it is safe to assume that offspring were produced out of those unions. What the names of these "intermediate" racial groups should be would soon become an issue. One of the names that surfaced for one segment of America's emerging mixed-race population was Black Indians. I bet most of you reading this are hearing that term for the first time, and so you might be thinking, "What happened to those people and where did they go?"

23. Clarke, *Christopher Columbus and the Afrikan Holocaust*, 84.

24. Jones, *A Dreadful Deceit*, 295.

In 2018, African American basketball superstar Kyrie Irving went through an "Indian" naming ceremony. Kyrie Irving has more than likely always checked the box that said black, or African American, when asked to identify his race on any official document. But that understanding was shaken to its core. The ceremony changed Kyrie from being simply black into a Black Indian for the first time in his life. As a reporter noted, "In an emotional naming ceremony, Boston Celtics star Kyrie Irving was given the Lakota name Little Mountain by the Standing Rock Sioux tribe . . ."[25]

Mr. Irving's mother was part Sioux and, as with most American blacks, the government forces you to be African American, or black, regardless of what combination of blood is flowing through your veins. Mr. Irving said, "It's really special for me to be here because I lost my mom at a very young age, and I had no idea about the history and how inclusive this group is and what it means to be part of the Sioux tribe."[26] Wow, Mr. Irving just raised the possibility that when people-groups see the world organically, as Native culture does, then it is possible to see humanity as one interconnected, organic whole.

Who am I—Who are You?

Beginning with America's founding the society was structured with racial division as the norm and so it should not be surprising that it has persisted to this day. Law professor Ian Haney Lopez writes, "In its first words on the subject citizenship in 1790, Congress restricted naturalization to white persons."[27] This means that from its inception, people in the United States understood that to be American was to be white. Everyone else was labeled as some type of other. For this reason, there are people who have never been that open to granting white status to offspring that resulted from interracial intimacies. Later on, laws were written to ward off the possibility of the humanizing of dark babies. It was called the "one-drop rule." The one-drop rule essentially mandated that any person with even one drop of African blood was a Negro. The end result of that rule meant that anytime a child was born with even a small percentage of Negro "blood," the child would still be a Negro.

25. Windhorst, "Kyrie Irving," line 1.
26. Windhorst, "Kyrie Irving," line 17.
27. Lopez, *White by Law,* 1.

Evidence that this mind-set lingers on can be seen in the way that our society perceived the "race" of Barack Obama. I could not find one article that referred to him as white, but plenty that referred to him as black. There were several that said he was "mixed race." But if that were true, and his racial mixture was 50-50, logic would dictate that each of the parent's race should be reflected in the way he was labeled. That means that I should have found a good percentage of writers that viewed him by his "white half." Since I could only find articles that referred to his 50 percent black heritage, it seems obvious to me that his 50 percent white heritage did not count.

The naming of the "mixed raced" people by Spanish colonizers of the Americas is a perfect example of the way abuse of labels results in more confusion instead of less. Pedro Alonso O'Crowley listed some of the new names that the "racially pure" Europeans assigned to the differently hued people that they had conquered. As you read these names think about how much effort was expended to create the impression that humanity is not one interconnected whole. "(However) It is agreed that from a Spaniard and a Negro a mulatto is born; from a mulatto and a Spaniard, a morisco; from a morisco and a Spaniard, a torna atras and from a torna atras and a Spaniard, a tente en el aire. The same thing happens from the union of a Negro and Indian, the descent begins as follows: Negro and Indian produce a lobo; lobo and Indian, a chino; and chino and Indian, an albarazado, all of which incline towards the mulatto."[28]

What is a mulatto, and what does the term imply? In the US it would mean blackness, and once African blood is introduced into a family's lineage, the offspring never really escape the stigma attached to being black. As Mr. O'Crowley observed in 1774, "It is known that neither the Indian nor Negro contends in dignity and esteem with the Spaniard; nor do any of the others envy the lot of the Negro, who is the most dispirited and despised."[29]

The following story illustrates the extent to which mixed race people would go to avoid being named one of those dispirited and despised colored persons. Many lighter-skinned people would "pass for white" by hiding their parentage. Recently I watched a white author named Gail Lukasik being interviewed by Megyn Kelly. Ms. Lukasik had written a book titled *White Like Her* and discussed the time when she learned a family member's birth certificate said white, and the death certificate said black. The author offered the interviewer a tongue-in-cheek observation by saying, "He

28. Katzew, *Casta Paintings*, 192.
29. Katzew, *Casta Paintings*, 192.

came into the world white and died black—I am not quite sure how that happens."[30] Think about that for a second. What would have happened to her had her blackness been found out? Would the old one-drop rule kick in, or is there a statute of limitations on selecting race? Would the way we do race in America to this day, as evidenced by the way President Obama was labeled, mean she would have had to reclassify herself at the next census? Interesting, is it not?

It is worth highlighting that improperly named interracial bodies have been able to move in and out, and in between the fixed and immutable racial categories established by the government. Then consider for a moment the many relationships that flourished between people not knowing the race of the other. They were able to love each other in spite of the fact that had their partner's race been known, they would have had nothing to do with them. So many decisions in life are made because of our society's commitment to the existence of different (separate) races, and for what?

Vivian Chou observed, "Ultimately, there is so much ambiguity between the races, and so much variation within them, that two people of European descent may be more genetically similar to an Asian person than they are to each other."[31] Activist Woullard Lett stated ,"The human genome has been sequenced and it has been established as the scientific consensus that 'race' as a biological category, a genetic typology or a scientific reality does not exist."[32] Please consider for a moment the number of lives that were shattered, and the amount of blood that was shed, all because some were insistent that different races did exist.

Own the Name

Earlier in this chapter I discussed Muhammad Ali. As we close this chapter, let us look at the man that Mr. Ali fought to regain the heavyweight championship, George Foreman. George Foreman named his five sons George! Mr. Foreman gave these reasons for the unusual choices, "I named all my sons George Edward Foreman so they would always have something in common. I say to them, if one of us goes up, then we all go up together, and

---

30. Youtube.com, "Meet the Woman."

31. Chou, "How Science and Genetics Are Reshaping the Race Debate," para. 10.

32. Lett, "Readers Respond," line 11.

if one goes down, we all go down together!"[33] All I can say to that is, yeah George, that is how it should be in many areas of our society.

In the United States a person cannot copyright a name for the purpose of exclusive use unless that name is an established commercial entity. Why have that law? To prevent others from creating products that bear the same name but are markedly inferior. God's name is to be above all names, but how can we prevent competitors from using that name in a way that is essentially different from the original? Maybe that is the fundamental issue addressed by this command. At the time it was given, the name of God was to have a unique and special place above all other names. That is the crux of this Commandment. Why? Certainly not due to any insecurity on God's part—but because a name really mattered! This chapter highlighted some damage that naming human beings by race has done. As Paul Louis Metzger and John Morehead note, "Names do matter, but all the more important are relationships that put flesh and blood and stories to names."[34] When it comes to race, it is time for a new story to be told.

33. Quinn, "George Foreman," line 11.
34. Metzger and Morehead, "What's the Big Deal?," para.12, line 15.

5

Remembering

Remember the Sabbath Day and Keep It Holy— Be Holy for I Am Holy (Exod 20:8–11).

I have a fond memory of demanding that my parents explain why I had to go to church *every* Sunday. Their answer was not philosophical and they did not attempt to sell me on the idea of going because I would eventually learn to like it. What I was told was that I was going to church every week at 11 AM because one of the Commandments reads, "Remember the Sabbath Day and keep it Holy." Young Jimi took that to mean that church attendance was not a matter of choice, personal piety, or even a Christian entertainment option—it was a duty, and off to the back seat of the car. Fast-forward to the 1990s.

One day I was having lunch with a fellow pastor, and he asked, "Do you teach your congregation that it is okay to go anywhere on Sunday other than church?" Shamefully, I responded to his serious and sincere inquiry with an inappropriate smirk. To this, my friend smiled and said, "No Jimi, I am serious." My pastor friend in Belize was not the first person to take the Sabbath day very seriously. It may surprise you to learn that early Virginia law contained statutes requiring its residents to attend church twice on Sunday and do nothing else. The punishment for those wanting to sleep in and watch the Super Bowl was: "Upon pain for the first fault to lose their provision and allowance (food and other basic necessities) for the whole week following; for the second to lose the allowance and also be whipt;

48

and for the third suffer *death*."[1] I would assume that the majority of today's Christians are not concerned at all about remembering the Sabbath. In fact, I doubt many would even see the concept of a Sabbath rest as being a necessary component of their faith journey. However, since it is included in the Ten, maybe we should, only not to the level of the early Virginians.

Let us look at the way people who were alive at the time Moses received this Word may have observed Sabbath. Philo of Alexandria, a first-century Jewish historian and philosopher, wrote, "What then did [Moses] do regarding these seventh days? He commanded them to assemble together in the same place, to sit with one another with order and reverence and listen to the laws."[2] Philo's observation implies that those people may have understood this Word similar to the way my friend and my parents did. You are to go to church on Sunday, and that is that. However, for many religious Jews, the Sabbath meant a complete withdrawal from the normal day-to-day activities of life and resting. Let us address another misperception that could find its way into our thinking when the word *Sabbath* is heard. The people Moses spoke to knew not to get caught up in leisure activities that would prevent them from honoring their religious commitment. They were a nomadic tribe of people in rocky and barren desert terrain, and their distractions were probably few. For this reason, it may be better to think that Moses instructed the people to find a place to gather, instead of a group traveling to a place to meet, such as a church building. A part of Sabbath rest is developing an awareness of the presence of God as much as it is the energy spent seeking him in a specific place.

Let us accept the premise that people alive today are expected to "remember the Sabbath" the same way as times past. Perhaps the first question we should ask is, "What should be remembered?" Is it important to remember which day of the week is the only allowable day to hold a service? Maybe, but Seventh Day Adventists hold services on Saturday rather than Sunday, believing Saturday is more in line with the historical practices as recorded in the Torah. Now consider this definition for a Jewish Sabbath, "A weekly 25-hour observance, from just before sundown each Friday through the completion of nightfall on Saturday."[3] That definition may not exactly jibe with the day the Seventh Day Adventist belief to be closest to the Jewish Sabbath. The next question is whether one space is more appropriate

1. McFarland, "Sunday Laws in America," para. 2.
2. McGowan, *Ancient Christian Worship*, 69.
3. Myjewishlearning.com, "Shabbat 101," para. 2, line 1.

than another to hold services. Then we could discuss whether or not any particular worship style is holier than another. See where I am going? It is not always easy to obey what on first hearing seems to be a straightforward Commandment.

How We Remember

What if one of the keys to unlocking this Commandment was located in the memory? Think about the way we use the word *remember* in common speech. Here in Texas, "remember the Alamo" can be found written in schoolbooks, on store windows, and in tourist guides. So, could recalling a specific event be the first step in obeying this command? Then there is also the 9/11 slogan "never forget." Could it also be that in order to remember one must intentionally avoid forgetting? It is important to note that Judaism is a faith that is grounded in remembering by the retelling of its history with God over and over. Greek philosophers such as Aristotle and Plato saw memory as primarily a function of the brain and intellect, meaning remembering is a matter of thinking about a particular subject or event.

Contrast that with the way the Jewish people remembered their God. They devoted a great deal of time and energy to developing liturgical practices that would infuse their history with God into the very core of their being. Protestant ethicist Reinhold Niebuhr had this to say about this form of remembering: "A basic distinction may be made between various interpretations of the meaning of life by noting their attitudes towards history."[4] He warned that those who exclude history miss the "fuller disclosure and realization of life's essential meaning."[5] Many of us are familiar with the almost clichéd maxim that says that people who ignore the mistakes of the past are certain to repeat them. I would say there is another reason history is a vital component in the formation of morals. That is because as a pastor I have heard people in the congregations where I served hold somewhat "goofy" theological positions because they expected things from God that an honest reading of the lives of past Christians would simply not support.

4. Niebuhr, *The Nature and Destiny of Man Volume II*, 2.
5. Niebuhr, *The Nature and Destiny of Man Volume II*, 2.

What We Remember

The church I attended as a youth was 100 percent black, while the churches I have worked in since have been 90 percent white. Why is that important? Is it your understanding that a mono-ethnic church is somehow more God-honoring than a multiethnic church? Or do you see people of one ethnicity, or race, worshiping together as really not a bad thing? Perhaps this next sentence will help us rethink how we "member" sacred spaces. My friend Dennis Marcellino quipped that if churches remain as segregated as they are now, then we should rename the days that white churches meet White Sabbath, and the days when black churches gather Black Sabbath. Yes, Black Sabbath is the name of a popular 1970s English rock band. And I know that his suggestion was meant to be funny, but in many ways, his joke was pretty insightful. The band was named after a Boris Karloff horror film. If church attendance reflects the way racial groups are interacting with each other, then it appears there are many who are horrified at the prospect of attending church with a different ethnicity.

Sacred spaces can almost become battle zones when they mirror the way the culture organizes itself rather than being an alternative to it. If a component of Sabbath observance does center around church attendance, then maybe we should give more thought about how we "member" them. There is one given within the church growth community, and that is that people feel more comfortable associating with others like themselves. They use this as justification to decide who their target audience is when planting churches, and by extension, who their target audience is not. My question would be, who feels most comfortable with whom and why? If we say being comfortable happens along racial lines, would this not be an idealized view of the way people with the same skin color have gotten along with each other over time? Think about it. Additionally, that presupposition automatically produces a form of dis-membering that creates a church that reeks of partiality and neo-racist predilections. Instead of the church being a place that intentionally includes outsiders, these types of churches only focus on serving people like themselves—the saddest part might be that they celebrate it.

How You Welcome

No matter how many times a slogan like "We welcome you" is placed on a banner around a church, or on its website, there are many other things happening that communicates "stay out." I used to go out to nightclubs to hear bands with two white friends, Andy Jacobs and Sydney George. There was this one particular club in Los Angeles that used a dress code to keep black people out. We were unaware of the practice, and one night we decided to check out a band that was playing there. We were about to enter when one of the doormen stopped me and said that I needed to be wearing a sport jacket. Andy, who was a frequent customer of the place, informed the bouncer that he'd been there several times without a sport jacket, and there was never a problem. The guy just said it was their policy and it was out of his hands.

Undeterred, we went back to my house where I grabbed a jacket, and raced back. When we arrived at the door, the guy said that I need to be wearing either dress pants or creased jeans. Upon hearing that Andy got mad and told the guy he'd been there many times in casual attire without a problem, and then asked to see a manager. The guy refused, saying that he was only following policy, and it was always up to the bouncer to decide appropriate dress. If you are white, you probably cannot imagine how many times people like myself have had to endure humiliation in these types of situations. You may even be thinking that my example was just one of those unfortunate incidents, and besides, how do I know that race was involved? If the last thought entered your mind, you should know that a decade or so later, that very chain was successfully sued for its discriminatory policies.[6]

The previous story illustrates the way many "stay out" signals can be sent to people of color that white people are completely unaware of due to lack of firsthand experience. Often times if a person of color points out the injustice it is met with polite skepticism by their white friends. If you are a white person who never sees any of racism's subtleties, consider this recent story from the world of sports.

John Henson, a professional basketball player, decided to buy a Rolex watch at an upscale suburban jewelry store. The store employees saw black men exiting a new Cadillac SUV and refused to answer the store's doorbell. Then the employees locked the door and ran to the back of the store and called the police. The employees can be heard on the 911 call giving

---

6. See Glanton, "Red Onion."

reasons why they were suspicious, with one of them being they did not look like "normal customers." The police became suspicious of the black guys in a new Cadillac as well and ran the license plate numbers without a traffic violation even having occurred. A short while later it was determined that John Henson was not only a legitimate customer, he was one with the means to pay for anything he wanted. Even after learning who the prospective customer was, the white employees wanted the police to stay there while he shopped.

If you are assuring yourself that nothing like that happens in your community or church, you are mistaken. I have recently experienced similar treatment at two predominately white churches where I was hired to be a pastor. Both times I was hired before people in the congregation knew that I was coming on staff. One Sunday I went to a church in Florida where I was to work, and not one person spoke to me other than the greeters. At another church where I was to be a pastor, someone followed me around the building as though he suspected me of being up to no good. Suspicion of the stranger must be purged from our churches if they are ever to be a model of the kind of peacemaking that leads to a Sabbath rest. It really is time for a change, and each one of us is "on the clock" to bring that about.

When?

I believe it is a safe assumption that we cannot understand God fully without allowing for some form of mystery. One of the more complex mysteries is our perception of time. Augustine asked, "For what is time?"[7] And then he followed up with an even more difficult question, "Who can explain this easily and briefly?"[8] Perhaps it is because I am an artist and a pastor that I can relate to this answer to St. Augustine's question: "There is no time in itself, rivaling God and imposing conditions on him."[9] We allow our busy lives to do just that, impose conditions on us. As we have discussed, people of faith argue about whom to invite, and where to observe the Sabbath, but it is equally important to consider when. This is why. According to a website dedicated to the philosophy of time, the Greeks had two different words for time: "Chronos refers to numeric or chronological time, while

---

7. Augustine, *Confessions*, 230.

8. Augustine, *Confessions*, 230.

9. Begbie, *Theology, Music, and Time*, 93.

another word Kairos refers to the more qualitative concept of the right or opportune moment."[10]

The Greek understanding of time is the basis for the way we perceive time. Consider this way of understanding time: "God is not subject to the laws of nature, he is not subject to measured time. He does experience a temporal now, somewhat as we do, but his intrinsic experience is not measured by regular, law-like intervals."[11] That is important to us for two reasons. The first being God is time, "He experiences temporal succession, but this succession is that of the progression of his own consciousness and actions rather than that of any external constraints."[12] That suggests that if we follow suit and free ourselves of constraints, anytime would be the right time to invite someone into a Sabbath-type of relationship with you. That means that we should be as loving and accepting of people in public spaces as we are to people at church. Said another way, Sunday is not the only time to be tenderhearted and compassionate towards others. Every day is the opportune time.

Torah prescribed for certain events to happen at certain time periods, thereby establishing a rhythm for the Jewish people to live out God's assignment for them. That is why their religion is chock-full of feasts, festivals, and ongoing ritual. Those prescriptions were not given by an arbitrary and capricious God who was desirous of spoiling everyone's weekend. They were given as a tool to bond people together, and bring hope to those on the outside. Jesus said the Sabbath was made for man and not the other way around. Sabbath is a time of togetherness for those feeling estranged from God due to the challenges of life. I find a similar sentiment in this saying, "Zohar asserts as valid for all times that God, Torah, and Israel are at one."[13] We plan our lives around time in a futuristic sense. The future is not when a relationship with God should happen, nor is it when racial reconciliation should happen. They both can and should be happening in the present tense. The appropriate time to seek justice and reconciliation is a simple, but emphatic, now! It is in the pursuit of "oneness" that we keep the Sabbath because that is when we "worship the Lord in the splendor of his holiness."[14]

10. Exactlywhatistime.com, "Ancient Philosophy," line 7.
11. Iep.utm.edu, "God and Time," section 7, para. 2, line 7.
12. Iep.utm.edu, "God and Time," section 7, para. 2, line 9.
13. Fackenheim, *To Mend the World*, 327.
14. Ps 96:9, NIV.

6

Sources

Honor Your Father and Your Mother (Exod 20:12).

ENGINEER TURNED MICROBIOLOGIST DOUGLAS Axe opens his popular book *Undeniable* with what he calls "The Big Question." That is, "To what or to whom do we owe our existence?"[1] This chapter will not answer that question, but we will use his basic idea as a springboard to discuss the fifth Word. Let us start be rephrasing Mr. Axe's question regarding the source of our existence by replacing existence with morality and ethics. The big question then becomes, "To what or to whom do we owe our [set] of morals and ethics?" Before we address that question directly, I would ask that you accept the premise that everything that exists has a source.

Recently a British television special featured a Turkish family that walked on all fours.[2] They ambulate in a fashion similar to that of monkeys and apes. Evolutionary scientists automatically assumed that their unusual mode of walking was the result of backward evolution.

Whether or not they walk that way because of some evolutionary throwback—or because they mimic what their ancestors picked up from a monkey—is not important to our discussion. I mention them because at some point one of those family members is going to have an "aha" moment and stand erect. She or he will begin to walk upright, realize it takes much less energy to walk in that manner, and the two-legged revolution will be

---

1. Axe, *Undeniable*, 9.
2. Youtube.com, "The Family that Walks on All Fours."

on. That person would then become the source for the family's new and improved mode of travel. It is reasonable to assume that the first person to discover this will become a hero. In our society, the first person to create, invent, or discover something is celebrated, honored, and from then on considered to be the source. That happens in athletic competitions, scientific discovery, and even rock and roll.

Beginnings—Everything Has One

Many argue that the source for the majority of The Rolling Stones' early hits was not guitarist Keith Richards but Chuck Berry. My peers in the rock music world often joked that Chuck should be entitled to a healthy portion of their royalties. Should being the source of a good idea automatically entitle the originator to control what happens to it in the future? Maintaining the right to control intellectual property is fairly routine, and maybe the creator should have the same right to "control" the way we live out Christian ethics. My friend Leon Patillo once sang that Jesus came into the world to show us how to live. Jesus also came into the world to show us how to love. Love is both the source of and purpose for Christian ethics. Our willingness to follow Jesus is all the control he asks for or needs. If Keith Richards did use many of Chuck Berry's musical ideas as his own, maybe we should follow his lead and use more of Jesus' practices as our own.

Do What You Know

A. Kevin Reinhart offered the following caution: "To the historian of religion, chasing origins is of doubtful value because origins tell us nothing."[3] He continued, "It is more fruitful to ask: What is it about this question that fascinated?"[4] That intrigues me in light of where we currently are in terms of ethics. Let us take a look at a few current ethical challenges that I find fascinating before we address what may or may not be the best methodology for arriving at *the* proper ethical code. For those of you who have understood Christian ethics to be more closely related to personal piety than a Christian being socially conscious, hang on to your hats.

3. Reinhart, *Before Revelation*, 10.
4. Reinhart, *Before Revelation*, 10.

The ethical questions on our horizon emanate more out of scientific advancement than societal dysfunction. The questions many ethicists are asking today relate to things such as can we trust science, and if we say yes, how far should science be allowed to go? Scientists are now able to grow human brain cells on a plate beginning with just a single cell tissue, and independent of a person. Scientists have developed robots that can perform many tasks that were unheard-of five or ten years ago. Will society need to develop standards for what is and what is not robot abuse? Will the church even take on conversations of this nature? But it doesn't stop there. We now have sex-bots that are said to contain microchips making them capable of being sexually aroused and then respond to their "partner." What about those robotic lifelike sex dolls used in brothels? Even the conservative state where I live will soon have one. Today most of the focus is on "female" bots, but what happens if and when "male" bots flood the marketplace? What will a church that avoids ethics on a weekly basis have to say about that?

Do What You Can

Scientific advancements have produced a new breed of ethical dilemmas that previous generations only saw in science fiction movies. Today we face more challenges in the arena of medical ethics than ever before. That is because some believe that a scientist should be free to do anything possible as long as it facilitates human evolution, regardless of the means used to achieve it. My friend Rudy once alluded to the idea that the government owns the citizenry. Okay, let us run with that a little. Let me ask who owns your cells after you die. Should it be your family, the state, or the medical community? Recently we lost my closet friend's younger brother and to my surprise, the family had to wait for a state medical professional to make the decision to release his body to the family so they could plan funeral arrangements. In the world of the future can you imagine a scenario where the medical specialists would see it as ethical to extract cells from a body without the family's permission, if they believed doing so would lead to human progress?

Is that an ethical question to you or a political one? Shouldn't it be the responsibility of each person to designate in their will who owns their cells? Or should we take it for granted that it is within the purview of a government to decide? If you lean towards the latter, will it soon become necessary for attorneys to add body parts to a standard will? Next up in the list of scientific advancements is "gene editing," or gene splitting, a process that can be used to produce designer babies. Nobel laureate David Baltimore said, "We sense that we are close to being able to alter human heredity."[5] The sales pitch for that will be the elimination of birth defects, etc. But once a child's genetic makeup is modified, would that child continue to be viewed as an extension of its biological parents?

Let us take gene editing out of the picture and put some everyday flesh and bones on the question. How would you feel if your next-door neighbor could afford to order a child with a guaranteed genetic makeup that would produce a boy who at the age of 18 would be 6 ft. 4 in., have an IQ of 173, have the color eyes and hair of your choice, and would be a gifted athlete? Would that lead you to think about the ethics of genetic manipulation for commercial purposes differently? Did you catch that the gender in the hypothetical was male? In the world of designer babies, it may be naïve to assume gender selection would not become commonplace if allowed by someone's government. Should genetic manipulation become just another consumer product that is for sale to the highest bidder?

Do What You Should

There are a few more ethical dilemmas that could be with us soon. It may be possible to scientifically engineer robots with human characteristics ranging from intellect to sexual responses. Is it not reasonable to assume science would also be able to engineer a robot or another type of machine with a moral conscience? What would happen to moral reasoning if the source of those decisions emanated from a manufactured brain? Could that brain be held accountable or would the ethics produced in that scenario be given a pass, using the proverbial garbage-in–garbage-out rationale? Would it be good medical ethics to have the human brain preserved after the body dies and the contents programmed in to a computer? Would the right to privacy be a thing of the past if every thought that a person ever had could be made available to the state, law enforcement, or the medical community after death?

What happens if the medical community convinces our society that we should question whether or not bodies are even needed or wanted. The great English physicist Stephen Hawking contracted a disease named ALS that caused him to lose his motor skills and speech over the span of a few

5. Theguardian.com, "Scientists debate," para. 2, line 1.

decades. It really is not hard to picture either the scientific community, or possibly, his family reaching a conclusion that the real Mr. Hawking existed in his brain and now that the technology allows us to preserve it, it might be better for all concerned to let the body die. Scientists are implanting genes into apes to make them smarter. When that is perfected, why not implant human brains in apes to help with manual labor, since they are stronger than humans?

The big question is what you think the source for tomorrow's medical ethics should be—or have you thought about it at all? We have just looked at a small number of scenarios that illustrate why a medical code of ethics based on utility may not be best. Religious ethics have no utilitarian goal beyond the one given to Abraham, and that is to bless others so they will follow suit and bless others.

Are We Not Bodies?

Mention of Stephen Hawking raises the issue of disability. From the Greek historical perspective, "Greek philosophy valued order, balance, and harmony in nature and society; disorder, as represented by morbidity and poverty, indicated a menace or curse to nature and society."[6] Present-day Westerners do not like disorder any more than the ancient Greeks did. Or said another way, Western people can harbor strong negative feelings for whatever it is they consider to be outside the "ordered" norm.

Pope Francis said, "Respect for the world begins with respect for the human body."[7] In spite of this strong statement by the leader of millions of Christians, there is another group of people that are forced into an isolated existence on the margins of our society because of their bodies. I call this group the differently abled, and for most of us, they are invisible to us as we live out our lives. The perception of them being somehow "abnormal" could be the reason many are indifferent to the way people living with a disability are treated. When was the last time you turned on the news and the newscaster led with a lament about the treatment that a differently abled person received? If a disabled person is ever mentioned in a news story, it is about an act of kindness that a good-hearted able-bodied person performed for them. The differently abled person is often portrayed as an unfortunate or pitiful victim in need of sympathy rather than love.

6. Brock and Swinton, *Disability*, 24.
7. Vaticannews.va, "Respect for the World."

Our culture's preference for the "body beautiful" makes it easy to understand why this people-group is consistently marginalized. But why do people of faith recoil from having conversations about disability in the church? Why is an organization founded on love, the church, often extremely unloving towards these people? One reason is probably found in a misperception about what disability is and what it means. For most of us disability is viewed medically, and in the words of Thomas Reynolds, that "tends to reduce disability to a problem requiring diagnosis and treatment, a broken object to be fixed, made better, or overcome."[8]

Body Beautiful

Today's emphasis on positivism in the church has led many to see disability as not being a medical problem but a sin problem resulting from the fall. Throughout the history of the church there has been a scramble to come up with a "logical" explanation for why this population exists. We would prefer an explanation that would allow us to hold on to the belief that God is good, even though if we were more honest, we know that we may have doubts if we happen to run into a blind person with a severely deformed body. Many Christians have decided to resolve this possible paradox the way the ancient Greeks did. They develop a parallel source to explain why this people-group clearly outside "the norm" exists, saying that, "diseases, injuries, and malformation were signs of ill will by the gods."[9] Of course as Christians we deny the existence of other gods, but we are more than willing to allow for the possibility of a fallen angel being responsible. That is because we are convinced that it is our right and responsibility to define human perfection and not God's.

Many Christians are quick to say that God is in control in every situation and circumstance, but will stop short of saying that God is in control of disability. It is time to admit that it is difficult to pinpoint the reason why people vary in appearance. Perhaps a better use of time might be to find out why we have used the existence of variety within the human species to exclude in the first place. It is time to take ownership of the pain we have inflicted by excluding some people created by God and admit that human division is "on us." Meaning the bent towards exclusionary behavior is not a natural tendency fobbed off on us by our genes or any form of external

8. Reynolds, *Vulnerable Communion*, 25.
9. Brock and Swinton, *Disability*, 24.

pressure. The majority of the exclusionary social "isms" that people hold up as proof of innate difference are elective in nature—we choose which one to use to dislike the other. Once we acknowledge that we exclude people by choice, it might be possible to understand that "Jesus community includes the broken and the destitute from the start, thereby bringing wholeness to what was alienated."[10] Aristotle said, "Some things are in their nature choice worthy"[11] and I believe that the acceptance and inclusion of the disabled, regardless of the severity of that disability, is one of those types of choices. The people whose body configurations disqualify them from being included in everyday life are also viewed in juxtaposition between normalcy and abnormality. They are not just outsiders; they are not considered to be viable possibilities for inclusion.

Are They Not Men?

Several years ago, my friend Eddie Tuduri introduced me to a guy named Lenny Capizzi, who wrote a song called "The Monster Mash." The song was a spoof on a popular movie at the time named *Frankenstein*. The plot of the movie centered around a doctor who sought to create life in his laboratory. Dr. Frankenstein's creation turned out to be a white male whose body was constructed with cadaver parts salvaged from hospitals and cemeteries. Why was the color of the body parts important if the goal was to create life? Our culture has always viewed the white body as the standard that automatically deserves elite status. So, it is little wonder that the mad scientist who created the monster restricted himself to using only white body parts. Perhaps his thinking was that to select any body parts other than white would make his creation ugly.

A Wikipedia article noted that when the plan backfired, what was created would be referred to as, "wretch," "monster," "creature," "demon," "devil," "fiend," and "it"[12] by the doctor. Not one of those words suggests beauty, and not one of them would be affixed to something deserving of honor. In fact, in the movie it was determined that the monster was unfit to have a place in society and so they locked him up. My experience has shown that many view the differently abled as being somewhat "monster-like" in appearance. We hide them away in various places. When we do

10. Brock and Swinton, *Disability*, 224.

11. Bobonich, *The Cambridge Companion to Ancient Ethics*, 113.

12. Wikipedia, "Frankenstein," line 20.

encounter one, we see them as an oddity and not a person in a different package. In our market-driven society, packaging, or how we dress a product up, is a very important component in how successful a product will be. I certainly know that the way something looks can be the deciding factor when purchasing a home, a car, or food. My guess is most of us evaluate just about everything by sight, but when it comes to race and disability, we tell ourselves we can somehow rise above the habit. I don't think so! The answer to the problem is probably found in being honest with ourselves that we do judge by sight, and then address the decisions made following those sight-based evaluations. Later in the book, I will introduce you to three of my friends that might help you see this wonderful group of people in a different way. But for now, let us continue our discussion about sources.

Honoring the Source

There are reasons for the genealogy of Jesus in the Gospels. One of those is that the sources from which a person descends often influence who it is they become. Even Darwin thought the sources of human descent important enough to title his book *Descent of Man*. The ancient Romans put a great a deal of stock in the family birth order as well. Listen to Cicero's words about what Romans perceived to be the source of their religion: "Privately they shall worship those gods whose worship they have duly received from their ancestors."[13] Later, the Medieval European monarchies existed because those governed accepted the idea that "royal blood" descended from a source created by God. When royal blood was passed on to succeeding generations it was believed to deliver the elements that legitimized a perpetual aristocracy that the subjects willingly honored.

Honoring one's extended family tree matters because they could remind a person about their connection to a long list of unknown relatives that walked the journey before them. Think back to any time period in history, such as 500 AD, 500 BC, or even 1000 AD. Each of us is related to someone who was alive at that time. It is amazing to consider that a portion of his or her genetic material has been passed on to us. Think of that another way. All Souls' Day is a holiday that many Christians around the world celebrate. They set aside time to remember those who have departed. Paint an imaginary picture of your relatives who were alive during those time periods. Think of their world views. Think of the political systems that

13. Bediako, *Theology and Identity*, 21.

existed during the time they were living. Consider the attitudes they may have had about their place in the world. And finally, the spiritual beliefs they held. Now consider what it was that you visualized about those unnamed ancestors, and further assume that they contributed to making you who you are. That is why the Bible stressed the importance of genealogies in the books Luke and Matthew.

The genealogies in the Bible also serve a broader purpose than simply providing information. They should remind people who are alive at any time period that they have a longer history encoded in their genes than one or two generations. Everyone in prison started out as someone's good kid. Many come from what would be described as a good family. We all know a family that has a "rotten apple," or what some people call a "black sheep." Where did that person's aberrant behavior originate? Biologist E. O. Wilson acknowledges that there is a conundrum here: "Few questions in biology are as important as the evolutionary origin of instinctive social behavior."[14]

British geneticist Alan Rutherford comments, "The most important story our genes tell is that we are all family, despite race or tribe; and why it's not our genes that turn people into mass shooters."[15] But what if the choices made by unknown, and long deceased, ancestors play a larger role in plotting the direction of our lives than we assume? What if a person's present behavioral tendencies are the result of genetic influence from their past? I cannot scientifically prove that it happens, but I can share a personal anecdote to illustrate that it could in fact happen.

I was raised with the understanding that my maternal grandmother's first cousin was a famous jazz saxophonist who died at an early age due to drug and alcohol abuse. That grandmother was married to a pastor and neither of them missed church or took a drink. My parents followed in that family tradition. My older brother William and I came along during the early years of the rock and roll rebellion in America. William and I were musically inclined, and we would both become involved in learning instruments and playing in bands. I am not sure if this happened to my brother, but I was repeatedly told that playing an instrument was fine as long as I kept my nose clean and did not end up like my famous relative. As fate would have it, William and I were playing in bands in the San Francisco Bay Area when drugs became a staple of the rock lifestyle. William and I were raised in the same household, the same way, and like many younger

14. Wilson, *The Meaning of Human Existence*, 61.
15. Worrall, "Why Race is Not a Thing," para. 2, line 4.

brothers I copied everything he did. However, that stopped with drugs and alcohol. For some reason my brother was able to sample those substances and then leave it there. He just wasn't interested in them. But I loved it on first "sip," and I tended to overindulge. The question is why me and not William? Was I morally weaker, or lacking the character to drink in moderation? Or, did I "catch" a genetic sequence from my first cousin twice removed that led to my love affair with alcohol?

Every word written in this chapter was written with the firm belief that everything that exists has a source, meaning a beginning, or an origin. St. Augustine said it this way, "Anyone anywhere who is born a man . . . no matter how unusual he may be to our bodily senses in shape, color, motion, sound . . . derives from the original."[16] The Word that we just discussed was given to remind us of the fact that if we were born via the traditional biological method, we have a source because we are all derived from two human beings. Cultural anthropologist Christopher Boehm noted in his book *Moral Origins* that Charles Darwin believed that not only did our biological existence originate with natural selection but our morality originated a similar way. Boehm wrote of Darwin, "He clearly thought our conscience and moral sense were as 'naturally selected' as our large brains, our upright posture, and our general capacity for culture."[17]

That just confirmed my earlier statement that everything has a source, even morality. Economist Adam Smith, the founder of capitalism, said, "In the process of making such judgements on a countless number of actions, we gradually formulate rules of conduct. We do not then have to think out each new situation afresh: we now have moral standards to guide us."[18] Christians do not have to think out each new situation afresh either, and that is because God is our eternal source.

16. Brock and Swinton, *Disability*, 72.
17. Boehm, *Moral Origins*, 6.
18. Adamsmith.org, "The Theory of Moral Sentiments," para. 12, line 1.

7

Respecting

You Are Not to Kill (Exod 20:13).

PHILOSOPHY IS THE STUDY of the way we interact with other human beings and the world around us. Theology is the study of the way we interact with God—which leads to right relationships with others and the world around us. Each of those disciplines anticipates the need for some form of a moral code to be in existence for human flourishing. The moral codes that philosophy advances are arrived at through human experience and reason. The morality drawn from theology is not dependent on human experience or reasoning and is external to both. Human history has made it crystal clear that conjoining reason-based morality with biblical morality into a seamless one has been difficult to achieve. The proof that this tension exists can be found in the ways we have viewed killing. Many people believe that the cosmos contains a universal moral code, with one of those universal laws being a prohibition against killing. Mike Lawrence, who was an ordained minister and skilled attorney, once said that if people worldwide cannot agree that killing is wrong, then there is not much hope for the world.

Let us look at how complex it is to arrive at an "obvious" prohibition against anything when different cultural traditions are factored in. Mike and I had a discussion about the actions of a Muslim father who was involved in some behavior that ran contrary to the ethics of our American culture. A family moved to the US to escape persecution in their home country. They had several children, including a preteen daughter. The family maintained their religious tradition and their cultural heritage in the

65

home—but also did their best to assimilate into American culture. Upon reaching high school age the daughter became Westernized and began to date a schoolmate. The family came from a society adhering to the strict discipline of arranged marriages. So it was a foregone conclusion that the daughter would marry within her faith. The fact that she was dating someone outside of her faith, and from a different ethnic group, was simply unacceptable. Her behavior was believed to be not just a sign of rebellion but a complete rejection of the family's values, and that was humiliating.

In response, the father and two of the sons beat the young woman until she vowed to return to the customs of her upbringing. That beating was severe enough to warrant a trip to the emergency room. When Mike and I learned of it, we discussed it and then shared the news with some friends. The differences between some of our perceptions led to some very heated philosophical discussions. Most of our friends were adamant that the family should be required to adapt to Western morality because they were living on American soil. A few questioned if holding them to America's Christian values was consistent with respecting the religions of others. What does freedom of religion mean if it does not mean freedom to exercise its precepts as understood by the majority of adherents? What does religious pluralism mean if the majority religion only allows a minority religion those practices that are compatible with the majority's? Can you see that the answer as to whether or not the family was wrong is not as simple as it seemed on first read?

Now listen to another story where the characters involved are also Muslim. My wife Julaine and I were very close friends with many people in the Bangladeshi community in Boca Raton, Florida. We had grown to love and respect them very much over the years and felt a deep sense of loss when we moved to Texas. One day prior to our move I had a casual conversation with a wonderful man named Rashid. He was a devout Muslim, a talented man, and an extremely hard worker. For those of you unfamiliar with Boca Raton culture, let me just say that the people there referred to a Mercedes Benz luxury sedan as a "Boca cab." Many of the young girls that went to school with Rashid's son had breast augmentation surgery and dressed in such a way as to make sure everyone was aware of how well it worked. Rashid could not understand why the families of girls of that age would allow their daughters to have that type of surgery and expose their cleavage to the degree they did.

I explained to him that our culture prides itself on teaching children to be an individual and autonomous "self." I told him that surgically altering their bodies was an acceptable way for them to express themselves. He shook his head and said, "Jimi, that's wrong." The question to you is, which method of parenting is the more moral or ethical? If ethics are not derived from a source external to one particular culture what other possibilities exist? In Western culture pragmatism, as determined by the outcome of an action, is certainly one possible source.

Violence for the Greater Good

Philosopher John Stuart Mill popularized the approach that whatever brought the most happiness to the greatest number of people would be the right thing to do. Consider the pragmatic approach to ethics in this hypothetical. Imagine that I am responsible for the safety of a small rural community in Alaska. Strict gun control laws have been enacted and yet the community feels extremely vulnerable. The reason for their angst is that for decades criminals would pick certain times of the year to descend upon the town and vandalize it. One day I happen to notice an ad for a type of gun that does not use the types of bullets prohibited by law. That is because they are not made from any form of metal but from an expandable synthetic composite. This new technology is not only guaranteed to penetrate the thick outerwear that the marauders typically wear—the bullets expand on impact, maximizing the damage inflicted.

The projectiles arrive and I decide that I should test them before the invaders attack again. In my mind the only sure way to test them is by actually shooting a person. I select the least liked resident in the town as my guinea pig. I shoot and kill a homeless man as he sits on a garbage bucket mumbling to himself in an alley behind a liquor store. Now I feel confident that the new bullets work! The residents of the town are happy with my test results too because I rid them of a troublesome drunk. In their view, the added bonus was that the efficiency of the new weapon also made them feel safer.

The mayor, the police chief, and other local officials decide not to call what I did murder. Instead, they characterize my target's demise as an unfortunate "collateral casualty" that occurred while making the city more secure.

This is an extremely unlikely hypothetical. However, it is not twisted logic. I presented it for the following reasons. The first is that once the Commandment is viewed as an abstraction to be analyzed rather than obeyed, we stop making the effort to find ways not to kill, and look for extenuating circumstances that will allow us to kill. More on that later. Second, the hypothetical exposes the possibility that "keeping us safe" can be a mask for many varieties of immoral killing, since security is something most people from every culture desire.

Justifiable Killing

Morality should not be a by-product of culture and it exists to hold it in check. One of the ways a society judges the morality, or immorality, of a violent act is by evaluating the relationship between the perpetrator and the recipient. Joseph E. David writes, "The relationship between law and violence is a fundamental problem that touches the most essential features of the concept of law and the understanding of its political and social function."[1] I presume that part of what Mr. David was referring to is the type of violence that may not result in legal prosecution. One example would be when someone, possibly a police officer, proactively kills to protect the community from a perceived potential offender. There are many people that would be saddened by the loss of life—but there are others who would assume the individual would probably be involved in criminal activity soon anyway and so it is understandable. Once that perception is in place, the killing becomes justified. It would not matter to them if the only "crime" the deceased had committed was mouthing off to the officer. The assumption would be, if the person had just complied with the officer, and kept his mouth shut, he would be alive today. Magically the death is no longer viewed as a killing but it is accepted as an appropriate punishment.

Consider this real-life example. A young unarmed black male was shot in the back while running away to avoid arrest. I am sure some of you are thinking innocent people do not run from the police. If that is you, please remember this Commandment is about killing, meaning it is not about crime and punishment. For additional context, the *Pittsburgh Post-Gazette* stated, "Pennsylvania law allows police officers to use deadly force to prevent someone from escaping arrest if that person has committed a forcible felony, possesses a deadly weapon or if the person has indicated he

1. David, *Jurisprudence and Theology*, 59.

or she will endanger human life or inflict bodily injury if not arrested."[2] A civilian captured the killing on video. According to a report:

> A bystander captured a video of the police shooting and posted it on his Facebook page. It shows two people running away from police cars, with their backs to the officers, as police open fire. "Why are they shooting?" the person who recorded the video said. "All they did was run, and they're shooting at them."[3]

I have read a story about a black security guard who had apprehended an armed suspect, detained him, and then waited for the police to arrive. When the police arrived, they immediately shot and killed the security guard! I read a few comments by witnesses at the scene that said the guard was wearing his uniform, including a hat with the word "security" clearly displayed. He was holding a firearm that he was licensed to carry as part of his job. It should not be difficult to understand why many in the black community would interpret the killing as follows. In spite of the security uniform, all the police saw was a black man with a weapon and they acted on that basis alone. This man worked as a security guard, was a church musician, and had aspirations of one day becoming a police officer. One other interesting sidenote to this tragedy is that this untrained security guard, by police department standards, was able to subdue and detain an armed suspect without needing to kill the person out of fear for his life.

Please do not misunderstand my point with all of this. I am not attempting to disparage the work law enforcement engages in on a daily basis. I am not even questioning the motives of police officers in general. My point is a much broader one. And that is, what do we think about the taking of human life by anyone? Secondly, it is becoming easier for us to justify killing when we believe that it was done for a greater good. In *The Rise of the Warrior Cop*, Radley Balko points out that in America's early stages of development there were no paid armed professional police. Law enforcement was a civil and community effort. When you read about a police shooting, do you ever wonder why America arms its officers, but the country that birthed it, England, does not?

Was America's decision to arm its law enforcement personnel due to the bad behavior of its citizens, or was it deemed to be a tool for controlling them? Perhaps it was because the government simply thought it best for

---

2. Lopez, "East Pittsburgh police officer charged for shooting," para. 8.
3. Lopez, "East Pittsburgh police officer charged for shooting," line 16.

each city to have something similar to what New York City Mayor Bloomberg said of his police department: "the seventh largest army in the world!"[4] Here is the problem with a mayor of one of the largest cities in the country making a statement like that. An army exists to fight the enemies of a country. A police department's stated purpose is to protect citizens and not fight them. What happens if one group of citizens are automatically perceived to be an enemy? That could lead to the problems that we discussed earlier, because as Mr. David also observed, "the political and social role of the law is to regulate violence,"[5] and I would add, not perpetrate it in order to defeat an enemy.

Nonlethal Killing

Have you ever given any thought to the differences in life expectancy between different ethnic groups living in the US? According to the United States Health and Human Services statistics, "American Indians and Alaska Natives born today have a life expectancy that is 5.5 years less than the U.S. all races population (73.0 years to 78.5 years, respectively)."[6] It is clear that on average Native people are prone to die sooner than other Americans. Why? One possible reason could be that the one people-group that has had their identity stripped from them, their culture demonized, then isolated on reservations, also had that inner will to survive killed in the process. One of the more unsettling government policies was the Indian Removal Act of 1830. That was a decision by President Andrew Jackson to uproot several Native tribes from their traditional lands and place them in the newly designated "Indian Territories."

That act of Congress led to the now infamous Trail of Tears. That was the name given to the journey the Natives made through a brutal winter to their new "homeland." An estimated four thousand human beings lost their lives as they were removed from the lands of their birth. It was the attitude of the United States government and its indifference related to the well-being of fellow image-bearers of God that ripped my heart open. This quote by one of the US generals at the time sums up what may have been

---

4. Balko, *Rise of the Warrior Cop*, 333.
5. David, *Jurisprudence and Theology*, 59.
6. Ihs.gov, "Indian Health Services (Disparities)," para. 4.

the prevailing view at the time. General Thomas S. Jesup said this in 1836: "The country can only be rid of them by exterminating them."[7]

I am sure that some of you are thinking, "How can the author make such a sweeping generalization about the attitudes of the settlers? He wasn't there." You are correct, I wasn't there, but I did grow up in the golden era of Hollywood's portrayal of America's Western expansion. Just this past week I watched a film that told the story of an actual Native chief named Crazy Horse. Crazy Horse "took up arms against the United States federal government to fight against encroachment by white American settlers on Native American territory and to preserve the traditional way of life."[8] One scene in the movie depicted the leader of a civilian wagon train questioning an Army officer about how safe it would be to travel west. The officer reassured the settler that they would be safe as long as Crazy Horse stayed on "his side" of a river and the settlers stayed on theirs. But the notion that the US government had the right to decide which side of a river belonged to whom illustrates the "attitude" that I spoke of earlier. Please understand that the producers of the film would not have characterized the events that way without knowing that a receptive audience awaited.

Killing Dreams

Consider some of the aftermath of what hundreds of years of nonlethal killing have done to an entire people-group. One example that comes to mind immediately is Native use of alcohol. It has been stereotyped and clichéd in such a way that minimizes the tragic results it has had on real-life families. Cherokee researcher David Patterson said, "The shame and abuse from historical trauma suffered by Native peoples, and the forced disconnection from culture and heritage, is a perfect setup that can lead to abuse to ease the pain."[9] I realize that many people will balk at the notion that pain can span generations, and that the residual effects of that pain can be passed down. However, many of those same people readily embrace the idea that American ingenuity, exceptionalism, and cultural pride can be handed down in the same manner. Should it not follow that if one is possible then the other must be too?

7. Dunbar-Ortiz, *An Indigenous People's History*, 97.
8. Wikipedia, "Crazy Horse," line 3.
9. Quoted in Bentley, "Alcohol," para. 8, line 5.

Dr. Patterson further said, "About 18 percent of American Indian or Alaska Native adults need substance abuse treatment, almost twice the national average, according to figures from the federal government."[10] Here are some troubling facts about alcohol use that will shed more light on one of my major points in this chapter. An article notes, "Problems continue among contemporary Native Americans; 12 percent of the deaths among Native Americans and Alaska Natives are alcohol-related."[11]

Another said that "Death rates for American Indians are similar to those of whites for most causes, but substantially higher for cirrhosis of the liver, and for injuries, suicide, and homicide."[12] Each of those can be the direct result of alcohol or exacerbated by it. A very troubling sidenote is that one of the myths I grew up hearing was during the settling of the West, Indians would trade land for "firewater" (alcohol). But the settlers decided that alcohol made Indians violent and stopped providing it for them. Thankfully I met some Native pastors that dispelled those myths.

The majority of us will live our entire lives without ever reflecting on what life on an Indian reservation is like. Yet, one in five indigenous Americans lives on one. A Native friend told me a story that illustrates just how tough life on a reservation can actually be. An elderly male froze to death in his home one winter because he lacked the funds to purchase what was necessary to keep him warm. When my friend shared the story, the point was not that the man died, it was that no one seemed to care. I have another friend named Cynthia, who is white, and she experienced reservation life firsthand teaching elementary school on one prior to becoming an Episcopal priest. She said of one of her students, "I tried to see how this student could succeed and live on the reservation; but the only way to succeed was to go away to school—and then you were exiled from your home and there was no job for you to return to. It was a lose-lose situation." That is the legacy that US policies have handed down, and those policies have only produced crippling despair and exterminated the hope of millions.

A Native high school student named Terry Redlightning offered this observation concerning the indirect effects of alcohol and how it can depress an entire community: "Only 17 of his 100 classmates at Flandreau Indian School graduated with him. He went on to say that there was a 'feeling of hopelessness' pervading his community back home and said Indians

10. Schwarz, "Overcoming Addiction," line 16.

11. Wikipedia, "Alcohol and Native Americans," line 1.

12. Prb.org, "Racial and Ethnic Differences," para. 2, line. 1.

there live on whatever comes to them."[13] The sense of "hopelessness" the young man described is a real-life example of why nonlethal killing can be just as brutal as any other form. Yes, these past few paragraphs are direct and are probably difficult to hear for anyone who reads them. However, once a people-group has been imprisoned on their historical homeland, it is difficult for them to believe there will ever be any form of relief until the wrongs done to them are fully and truthfully acknowledged.

Necessary Killing

When I was younger, it was common to hear people ask, "What nationality are you?" That is because at that time the Western world was organizing itself by independent and sovereign nations that had clear and distinct national borders. Canadian philosopher Graeme Nicholson drew a distinction between civilization and a nation. Civilizations are organic groupings of people, whereas nations are formed around a specific legal system and mission. For example, I have a friend in Belize City, whom you will meet shortly, whose people are the Maya. Notice I did not say that he was Mayan, but that his people are the Maya. That is because his tribal lineage transcends the borders that were drawn to create Mexico, Belize, and Guatemala, etc. My friend would identify much more with the people of his tribal heritage than he would with those holding citizenship papers from any particular government. That is why I believe Mr. Nicholson was on good footing when he wrote, "Civilization has always preexisted each historical nation."[14]

At the time the United States ratified the Constitution in 1788, there were only about twenty nation-states in the world. As of this writing, the number of nation-states has increased to more than 120. Most often when we think of morality, and ethical behavior, we do not think of them as applying to nation-states. We believe that an individual can be immoral, but we rarely describe a nation-state as *being* immoral—it can just commit immoral acts. When a country such as Germany committed a crime, the individual soldier who carried out the criminal behavior was put on trial and not the country. In fact, some of the soldiers involved in the atrocities of World War II used the "only following orders" defense in an attempt to shift the blame back to Germany. It did not work. However, what was interesting about that entire scenario was that the nation-state had the right to

13. Schwarz, "Overcoming Addiction," para. 21.

14. Nicholson, *Justifying Our Existence,* 135.

execute those very soldiers for treason if they had refused to follow orders. Apparently, they were on their own if there happened to be any negative repercussions that resulted from those orders.

So the question becomes, who is it that should be blamed when a nation-state kills? A famous Texas outlaw named John Wesley Hardin once bragged that he "never killed anyone that didn't need killing."[15] Yes, he was an outlaw and an antisocial menace who lived by his own rules. But what happens if the leaders of a nation-state make what might be characterized as a similar statement about someone they thought "needed killing"? If the average citizen was not consulted, or asked their opinion prior to the killing, are they in some way culpable?

A Japanese man named Tsutomu Yamaguchi worked in Hiroshima, the city where the first nuclear bomb in history was used. Keep in mind, the bomb was dropped on a city and not a military installation. Mr. Yamaguchi miraculously survived the bombing. The next day he returned to his home in Nagasaki. Then the unimaginable happened. Mr. Yamaguchi returned home in time to experience the fury of a second, larger bomb. Once more he survived! He later had this to say about his experiences: "I can't understand why the world cannot understand the agony of the nuclear bombs. How can they keep developing these weapons?"[16] One amazing thing about this story is that Mr. Yamaguchi died free of residual bitterness.

The killing of civilian men, women, and children was characterized as being necessary to end a war by a nation-state—meaning it cast it as a virtuous act of self-preservation. Perhaps the question that we should ask ourselves now is how much necessary violence should a Christian accept as simply part of life. What is viewed as proper and necessary killing by one group, can often be seen as a war crime by another. Can you see how easy it is for killing to become not only a virtuous act, but also a moral one in the eyes of some? I am pretty sure that given the right set of circumstances, many of us could adopt the mind-set that there are people out there that "need killing." But what if we were to accept the adage that God frowns on someone taking a life that they cannot replace? Then we might be more diligent about obeying the Commandment that says, "You shall not kill." Let us end with this truism. Respecting every person's right to live is one of the surest indications that we are respecting God and each other the way we should.

15. Famoustexans.com, "John Wesley Hardin," line 21.
16. Wikipedia, "Tsutomu Yamaguchi," para. 9.

8

Valuing

You Shall Not Commit Adultery (Exod 20:14).

THROUGHOUT MY LIFE, MOST people have understood that the best way to interpret this Word is as follows. One of the Ten Commandments is a prohibition against a male or a female engaging in sex outside of marriage. Modern sensibilities regarding gender and sexuality aside, adultery was about sex and only sex. However, the blanket application that I grew up with was not true throughout most of history, biblical history in particular. In the Gospel of John, a group of scribes and Pharisees came to Jesus and asked what punishment should be meted out to a woman caught in adultery. The fact that a male was not included in the inquiry was not an omission or oversight.

During my ministry I learned that "Adultery (sexual intercourse between a married woman and a man other than her husband [the biblical prohibition does not include sex between a married man and an unmarried woman]) is the only sexual offense recorded in the Ten Commandments."[1] I am certain that some of you might have become a little angry reading that. The thought may have entered your mind that the inequity in the rules is just another example of the way ancient laws were written by a bunch of narrow-minded, primitive, and unenlightened male clergy. Before we address that possible misconception, I would like to take you down a few

1. Myjewishlearning.com, "Adultery," para. 2, line 1.

streets in the city of rock and roll to see how women were treated in a world that was anything but narrow-minded.

Rock icon Jimi Hendrix named one of his musical projects *the Band of Gypsies*. The use of the word *gypsy* was apropos because it perfectly described the lifestyles of the majority of touring rock musicians of the era. I can attest to the accuracy of that moniker with confidence because I was one of them. The rock star lifestyle that I lived was best characterized as continuous travel and endless partying, that included a few hours spent performing music, and then back to partying. I will leave it to your imagination to arrive at the best definition for partying.

Please do not misunderstand what I am saying because the fact is that the vast majority of professional musicians work extremely hard. It requires time and dedication for a musician to develop their skills to the level that the music made appeals to people. That is often followed by long periods of financial instability before becoming successful enough to actually make a consistent living. That alone made it a difficult career path. The relatively few musicians that did enjoy a modicum of success were faced with touring schedules that forced them to be away from home as many as nine months a year. That's not a lifestyle for everybody. If life on the road did have its perks, they were traveling to the world's great cities and meeting interesting people—that was both fun and exhilarating. But at other times, it was a journey down a street ending with isolation and lonely nights.

Loneliness, though never mentioned directly, was included in every tour's itinerary. The first time a touring pro plays a city it is exciting. The second time, not so much. After a while each of a city's individual characteristics bleed into the next. At that point life becomes an endless cycle of airports, hotels, stages, and over time they are indistinguishable. Then it requires effort to know that you are actually in a different city. You may remember a popular television commercial that featured a rock musician at the end of a concert. In a moment of confusion, he uses the wrong name for a city where he was performing.

Was there any type of relief available from a routine that resulted in occasional confusion and some degree of loneliness? There sure was: drugs and women! But wait a minute, a drug is a commodity and a woman is a person. In a perfect world using people is immoral. True! But we are speaking about the world of sex, drugs, and rock and roll. At that time there were certain females who found the bad boy rock stars irresistible. That changed the definition of perfect.

Devaluing Women

Keith Richards of The Rolling Stones wrote an autobiography that was simply titled *Life*. In that well-written book Mr. Richards told many stories of what life was like on the road for the world's greatest rock and roll band, especially when it came to the women who were affectionately called groupies. He told stories about women waiting in line to be with one of the band's members, and others offering themselves to band members knowing full well that a particular musician was in a committed relationship. One example was an offer by a woman to one member of the band to "be his mistress forever."[2]

Allow me to share a couple firsthand examples of such behavior. I will be using the word "girl" in the examples because that was the age of most of the women at the time the groupie thing was fashionable, and so no disrespect is intended. One time a band that I was in, referenced in the first chapter, Gene Redding and Funk, toured the Pacific Northwest. One of the guys made the mistake of giving a girl on a one-night stand his home address. It was not long after we returned to California that he answered a knock on his front door to find that girl from Spokane, Washington, standing there waiting to be welcomed in.

Another example: A drummer friend of mine was dating so many women he needed to keep a log in his bedroom to remember which girl was scheduled at a specific time on a particular day. Then there were the girls who lived in many major cities that believed it to be their duty to service traveling musicians with no strings attached. One of those groupies was interviewed by a popular gossip magazine and she cited my bandmate's name as one of her favorites. That did not end well because while we were touring my friend's wife read the magazine and this resulted in him returning to a not-so-happy home.

The ethos of the gypsy entertainer was that life was a party as long as no one was getting hurt. We reached that conclusion because it was "just sex." The bottom line is that our attitude towards women ended with us using them. I think it fair to ask, has there been a time in the history of the Christian church when the prevailing attitude of some of the males in power was similar? Absolutely. The party lifestyle was not invented by rock and roll musicians. The book of Revelation makes a brief, but extremely unfavorable, reference to a doctrine taught by a group of Christians called the

2. Richards, *Life,* 294.

Nicolaitans. Those folks were said to have been party animals in the mold of the sex, drugs, and rock and roll hippie musicians we have been discussing. St. Augustine would say this about the founder, "Nicolas had prostituted his own wife and advocated men's having all women in common."[3]

Dehumanizing Women

Ed West notes that the Danish King Canute ruled that "if a man commits fornication (sex outside of marriage) with a woman he is to be condemned, but if a woman commits it she is to become a public disgrace and her lawful husband is to have all that she owned . . . and she is to forfeit her ears and her nose."[4] A medieval writer speculated that when a man is caught having sex with a woman in a church, "they (the people) are not so much upset with the violation of the woman, a true temple of God, as by the breach of the corporeal temple."[5] Women were not sex toys, they were property, and as such they did not have many rights. Adultery was not a matter of betraying a committed intimate relationship, it was a violation of a man's property rights.

We fast forward in time a little to an era when honor codes were established. At that point women were not so much viewed as property, meaning a thing, but as a person that was also a private possession. In Italy, until 1981 a husband had a legal right to kill a wayward spouse.[6] The Pakistani version of honor killing included a husband having the right to kill an adulterous wife, and that did not become illegal until 2004.[7] The common denominator between each of these examples appears to be that a woman was never valued as a unique and special creation.

The 1960s brought a heightened awareness of the disparity in treatment between men and women. In the Western world the women's rights movement demanded an end to unequal pay. Domestic violence was no longer dismissed as being simply a family issue. Sexual harassment and sexual violence was not to be tolerated any longer. Those demands were legitimate and long overdue. That movement was comprised of educated white women for the most part, and their frustrations were heard loud

3. Bornstein, *Medieval Christianity,* 179.
4. West, *1066 and Before All That,* 46–47.
5. Abelard, *Ethical Writings,* 19.
6. Wikipedia, "Honor Killing," Italy section.
7. Wikipedia, "Honor Killing in Pakistan," section 4.1, para. 2.

and clear. But have you ever considered what life has been like for black women throughout their history in America? A PBS article stated that, "African American women had to endure the threat and practice of sexual exploitation."[8] Their life on slave plantations was one of fear and despair because "There were no safeguards in place to protect them from being sexually stalked, harassed, or raped, or to be used as long-term concubines by masters and overseers."[9]

I Take What I Want

The evil of American chattel slavery was more than simply forced labor. Think about the effect that seeing white men have sexual free rein of your women, including your mother, must have had on the African American male psyche. I grew up with the understanding that the etymology of the profane term *motherf***er* stemmed from a term the slaves used for the white men they had to watch use the women they loved and cherished. Over time, their attitude towards the privileges those white males assigned to themselves may have gone from hatred to envy, before landing on a twisted version of respect. In my neighborhood, the term *motherf***er* was not always derogatory. If you were to call the best athlete or musician around a "bad *motherf***er*," you were not belittling him, you were showing him respect. I do not share this version of how that term may have originated for shock value. I share it because it sheds light on the way slave women were treated that is in stark contrast to the film version of the happy, smiling, and compliant washer women or cooks.

African American men had to process the trauma of watching white males have unfettered access to any of their woman. Male slaves had to observe what could only be described as psychologically emasculating activities performed right in front of them—all while knowing that they would be hung or shot simply at the accusation that they had looked at a white woman inappropriately. This double standard was formulated by people that claimed they were establishing a Christian nation. I do not point this out to disparage Christianity in any way. Remember, I am an ordained Christian minister and I have given my life to that end. This is included to remind all of us that Christian values will not always prevent us from having moral and ethical blind spots. Sometimes blind spots can lead

8. Pbs.org, "Antebellum Slavery," para. 12, line 1.
9. Pbs.org, "Antebellum Slavery," para. 12, line 1.

to Christians being involved in some unconscionable behavior. A humble heart reminds us that we are all capable of similar errors. The Ten Words are not outdated slogans. They contribute to what makes us decent and we should never believe that we have evolved past them. That is because we could be involved in equally egregious behavior today and not even see it.

Brightest Eyes See the Clearest

I realize that many of you reading this would argue that slavery has very little to do with present reality related to race. If you are of that opinion then I would ask that you consider the current popularity of Ancestry.com and other sites that test DNA in order to trace one's genealogical roots. *USA Today* reported, "Genealogy is the second most popular hobby in the U.S. after gardening, and [on the internet] the second most visited category after pornography."[10] Human beings are naturally curious and they want to know their genetic history. They believe that knowing their genetic history offers insight into "who they are." Many of us are quite certain that genetic roots can impact and explain individual personality traits. We've all heard myths of Italian passion, or French intellectual sophistication, Asian discipline, etc.

Genetics also form the basis for why people perceive there are innate social commonalities among those of the same cultural lineage. For example, many Irish Americans assume that such a strong ethnic kinship exists that it is natural for them to prefer to associate with other people of Irish descent because of those shared cultural roots. Now consider the inherent difficulty that an African American family might have should they desire to trace their family heritage for a similar reason. It is very likely that should some people of African descent delve into researching their genetic roots what they might find would expose some unpleasant history. Let us suppose the search ended with them learning that one of their great, great, great grandmothers once belonged to a prominent white family across town. What would that knowledge achieve? One reality that people would rather not face is that America's white and nonwhite citizens have very different collective pasts, and those pasts have significance.

One additional hurdle for people of African descent to overcome in the pursuit of their genealogical history is that the records related to their family ties were rarely kept because that population was viewed as property

10. Rodriguez, "Roots of Genealogy Craze," para. 3, line 1.

and not people. In the US, African people were characterized as "a savage in Africa—a slave in America"[11] with little else recognized in between. Quite often whenever the topic of slavery comes up many white people are eager to point out that it is more important to learn who you are than who you were. Okay, but then why is tracing one's genealogy as popular as it is? Is it reasonable that as Americans we should take pride in our historical achievements, yet be unwilling to take ownership of the egregious sins committed against African people during the same time period? The harsh reality is that African women did suffer at the hands of their white "owners"! That ill treatment was not in keeping with the mores of a nation being founded on Christian principles. If you are white, I ask that you pause for a moment and think about whether or not there are inconsistencies about the way you view people of color around you today. Do you see them as one of you, or one of them? Should you desire to read more about what life was like for enslaved African women during that time I suggest you pick up a copy of *Sugar in the Blood,* by Andrea Stuart.

From Out of the Darkness Came?

For many people the mere mention of the word *Africa* conjures up negative imagery such as emaciated people with HIV/AIDS, or scantily clad aboriginals dancing in circles while progress passes them by. Or they envision piles of dead bodies that have been thrown into shallow graves as a result of endless tribal wars. In fact, for many years Europeans referred to Africa as "the Dark Continent," and developed myths about its inhabitants as being violent unsophisticated cannibals. Is that negative social identification really what Africa was and is all about? I cannot voice this strongly enough: No! Theologian Thomas Oden states, "Cut Africa out of the Bible and Christian memory and you have misplaced many pivotal scenes of salvation history."[12] I am sure some of you are not all that comfortable associating our Christian heritage with the continent of Africa, so let us dig a little deeper.

Mr. Oden lists the names of biblical characters whose stories were actually lived out on African soil. Listen to this list of names from *How Africa Shaped the Christian Mind*: "Abraham in Africa; Joseph in Africa, Moses

11. Yetman, *Voices from Slavery,* 45.
12. Oden, *How Africa Shaped the Christian Mind,* 14.

in Africa; Mary, Joseph and Jesus in Africa."[13] Then Mr. Oden cites several other names of people whose stories were lived out on African soil, ending with Augustine. Who was Augustine? Augustine is a saint in the Catholic Church, the Eastern Orthodox Church, and in the Anglican Communion, and he is referred to as being a "Latin Father and Doctor of the Church."[14] Although the Roman church claims him as a "Latin Father," he was from Africa. Notice how this Wikipedia article refers to his education as having happened in "North" Africa instead of simply Africa: "Augustine was born in present-day Algeria to a Christian mother, Monica of Hippo. He was educated in North Africa."[15] Look on a map and you will find that Algeria borders Mali and Niger, and both of those countries are called "West Africa." The tendency to label things to fit a certain perception exposes one reason why we know so little about our complete Christian heritage. In Western culture racial bias seems to play a role in everything, including our religious history.

To appreciate the seventh Commandment fully, it is imperative that we readjust our modern Western eyesight to acknowledge the continent on which both Judaism and Christianity were birthed. I am confident that sentence shocked many of you a little, but let us accept this different frame of reference as being true. Hopefully, a different perspective will help to see other ways to view women too. Much of human history has seen women relegated to being commodities, sex toys, inferior beings, possessions to control, and many other subordinate positions forced on them by the physically stronger gender. That was not always true on the continent of Africa. That is because several of the African societies were matriarchal. A matriarchal society is not simply the reverse of Western patriarchal society. It is a completely different way of structuring society. Women were valued in very different ways in Africa than in the West. It was much more than women functioning in roles traditionally reserved for men in the West—there was a completely different schema in use for deciding gender roles.

Valuing Women

I remember when the majority of media presentations depicted men as being the only gender capable of doing the things necessary for a society to

13. Oden, *How Africa Shaped the Christian Mind*, 14.

14. Wikipedia, "Augustine of Hippo," 11.

15. Wikipedia, "Augustine of Hippo," 11.

prosper. Women were portrayed as passive observers in the background supporting the men, and in some sitcoms of the 1970s, frustrating them. If we look to Africa, we can see that women have always filled roles traditionally assigned to men in Western society. Here is a current example: "Without any help from men, who were engaged in the battle many kilometres away, Saharawi women made a life in the refugee camps, where a section of the Saharawi population lives to this day. They have constructed tents, houses, schools and hospitals, as well as political, social and cultural structures."[16] Read Proverbs 31, which describes a woman presumably living on African soil through a matriarchal lens. You will see that the woman described in the text is industrious, a strategic thinker, an adept negotiator, and an excellent manager. The text does not imply that she possesses those abilities because of a husband but that she employs them with her husband. Quite a difference, wouldn't you agree?

With that in mind consider that the Jewish understanding of a woman's role closer to the time the Commandment was given. There were different assignments given to men and women, but that did not signal the inferiority of women and the superiority of men—it signaled a unique calling for each. I am asking you to listen to what follows through Jewish ears. Today there are sections within Orthodox Judaism that acknowledge matrilineal descent. In fact, "Virtually all Jewish communities have followed matrilineal descent from at least early Tannaitic (c. 10-70 CE) times to Modern times."[17] The Conservative Jewish Movement in particular embraces matrilineal descent because Isaac came from the maternal line of Sarah. Why is this important? Consider a definition of matrilineality:

> Matrilineality is the tracing of kinship through the female line.
> It may also correlate with a social system in which each person
> is identified with their matriline—their mother's lineage—and
> which can involve the inheritance of property and/or titles.[18]

The Jewish people, and by extension Christian people, are descendants of Isaac, the child of Sarah. Isaac was the firstborn son of Abraham and Sarah, and the father of Jacob. God changed Jacob's name to Israel and the Bible says that after the name change God blessed him. Why is this important? I want to make doubly sure that you understand that the people of

16. Dijkstra, "The Strength of Sahawari Women," line 15.

17. Wikipedia, "Matrilineality in Judaism," line 2.

18. Wikipedia, "Matrilineality," line 1.

Israel, the people-group called by God to be a blessing to the entire world, only exists because of a woman named Sarah. Sarah was called to become the mother of the promise, meaning the source of blessings to all nations. When speaking of *nations* here think people-groups, cultures, ethnicities, as well as nation-states. That could never have happened had one event run its natural course. Sarah was captured by an evil king and taken as his wife. Before the "marriage" was consummated, God speaks to this nonbeliever in a dream and says, "Don't touch her!" Then the king gives Sarah back to Abraham.

If we reframe the story and make Sarah the central character rather than Abraham, we might see a woman willing to do whatever it took to continue living—so that God's will would not be thwarted by a non-Hebrew king. Then, if we also reframe the way we look at Abraham, it could be that his lie to that king, was done to serve a higher purpose than just saving himself. It might very well be that everything done by this first couple of faith was done to save Sarah's life, to ensure that she would live to be the mother of the promise. In a world primarily controlled by men, using women in any way other than God's plan for *their* lives is sin. Let me be clear, both sexes can engage in adulterous behavior. That is not what I am talking about. What I am saying is, women are not the weaker sex to be conquered, exploited, or abused. Adultery by definition is an abuse of something, is it not? Whether you are a rock and roll musician, a married man in the workplace, or a person in a power position, such as a king, this Commandment says men are to value women, and not ever use them.

9

Thieving

You Shall Not Take from Others
What Belongs to Them (Exod 20:15).

My wife Julaine and I lived in Belize City from 1992 until 2000. We had only lived there a short time when I met a Maya man named Javier. We became friends because of a shared passion for martial arts, and soon we began to train together. I had brought some training videos with me when I moved to Belize City and I decided to loan one to him. One day Javier came over to train and I asked if he had the video that I loaned him. He said no, and added that he did not have it anymore. I then asked him was it lost or stolen. He said no to both. Then he let it be known that he had taken it to a karate school to show the students and left it there. He informed me that when he went back to the school someone had "taken it." This illustration exposes three of the more fundamental reasons why people steal: I see, I want, I take. And then they develop the ways, means, and justifications to make it happen.

I was raised in an American culture that sees taking something that doesn't belong to you as stealing, and so I believed it to be my duty to correct Javier. I said, "Do you mean someone stole it?" He returned the favor and corrected me with a firm, "No, someone took it!" I learned that day that in some cultures the responsibility of ownership lies solely with the owner. That means if you leave something for an extended period of time, it signals that you no longer want it and it is free for, in Javier's words, the taking. I would say that perfectly illustrates one of the truisms of the way humans form societies—people seem to grant for themselves intergroup "permissible theft." Consider this definition for the word *theif*: "a person who steals another person's property, especially by stealth and without using force or threat of violence."[1]

Imagine that you went to a farm in Nebraska to purchase some corn. You notice an old car in the corner of the family's barn. You look a little closer and realize it is a 1931 Duesenberg Model J Murphy that is worth twenty million dollars when restored. You ask the owner a few questions about that "old car" that is rotting away in his barn. He says that he has no idea what it is, it came with the property, and it has never run. Then you immediately offer to buy it for 10,000 dollars, and he accepts. Was that good luck for you, or was that stealing from him?

There are many ways that people exchange goods and services that could be described as unfair to downright thievery by some. When a community gets to define the word *steal* by its perceived needs, some types of taking from others will not be understood to be actual stealing. That is why I think it is important to define terms. I am defining *stealing* as unilaterally taking possession of something without permission. One example of an egregious violation of this Commandment was carried out by European kings and queens with the full blessing of some of the Roman Catholic popes. In the example of slavery, one group of people took another group of people captive and relegated them to "thing" status.

We acknowledge that forced servitude is ungodly, and yet there are many people who are reluctant to call America's slave system sin. Those who hold that view would prefer to describe slavery as being an awful time, and an unfortunate blight on history, but not sin. That spin on history has kept the American slave system relatively free from that much scrutiny related to the methods used to procure the free beings they enslaved. And what little is known about the capture and the ensuing confinement on the slave ships are rarely condemned for what they were. However, reggae superstar Bob Marley referred to that practice of trafficking human cargo as "stealing" from Africa.

Many might disagree with Mr. Marley's characterization of capturing a human being, and then setting up a system where that human being becomes a tradable commodity, as constituting a theft. Okay, what would you call it? Repatriation? Kidnapping? Holding prisoners of war? Forced

1. Lexico.com, "Thief."

immigration? Let me be clear, whatever rationale people created to justify slavery, it dehumanized the Africans. It stripped them of their culture, and robbed them of any form of human dignity. If you are deeply embedded in the romanticized version of America's founding as the introduction of democratic ideals of freedom and equality to the Western world, prepare yourself for a bit of a jolt. James Madison, the fourth President of the United States and "father of the Constitution," said this in 1774:

> If America & Britain should come to a hostile rupture, I am afraid
> an insurrection among Negroes may & will be promoted. In one of
> our Counties lately a few of those unhappy wretches met together
> & chose a leader who was to conduct them when the English
> Troops should arrive—which they foolishly thought would be
> very soon & revolting to them they should be rewarded with their
> freedom."[2]

I revisit this topic because the framers of the Constitution spoke of freedom and human rights but did not believe those freedoms should extend to Native and African peoples. Contradictions such as these are why many Christians can hold inconsistent views about what stealing is and is not. For example, I am sure many of you have heard sermons where the pastor put forward the idea that a person can "steal time" from her or his employer by slacking off at work. *Retail shrinkage* is a term used to describe the loss of inventory due to employee theft. Okay, most people do not steal items from product inventory you say? What about taking lightly used office supplies home, or padding an expense account? The typical response to any negativity regarding those forms of stealing is "everybody does it," as though that in and of itself changes the nature of the offense. That defense is also frequently in use when justifying one people-group robbing another of their dignity. If unchecked, that behavior will be understood by the overall culture to be normal.

Imagine that you are a citizen of Oxford, England in 1571. You have read about Holland and Spain's lucrative slave trading enterprises, but since you are an academic it has no bearing on your day-to-day life. The "everybody around you is doing it" attitude results in you, the everyday non-political Christian, not being able to recognize that some of the things your country is doing are actually a violation of this Commandment. Using that hypothetical as a frame of reference, please look at the European Age of Discovery. That is the doctrine that led to the conquest, and enslavement, of

2. Horne, *The Counter Revolution*, 19.

African people throughout North and South America. Think through the full implications of those practices as you read the way Emmanuel Chukwudi Eze characterized this time period:

> The beginnings of colonialism needs to be traced to both the sporadic and systematic maritime excursions into Africa by Europeans fortune seekers which began in the mid-fifteenth century. These commercial interests, individual as well as institutional, were aimed at the extraction and trading of gold, ivory, and other natural resources, and raw materials, but they quickly expanded into the exportation of able-bodied Africans and their children as slaves to the Americas and other parts of the world.[3]

Notice those enterprises carried out by the Europeans were not referred to as stealing, but as "extracting" and "trading." The selling of children into slavery was completely glossed over. Can you see how easy it is, when shared desires are in place, to allow garden variety gerunds to camouflage the intentional taking of something unilaterally?

To the Victor Go the Definitions

Allow me to restate my definition of stealing: "unilaterally taking possession of something without permission." Please remember that definition —especially the last two words, "without permission"—as you read the following illustration. Additionally, keep in mind how word usage might directly impact the way you interpret this hypothetical.

It is about five o'clock in the afternoon and I come to your house. I walk in and take your most prized possessions and then I drive off in your car. Outraged, you call the police. You give them my name as well as a detailed description of everything taken. A few hours pass and there comes a knock at your door. You peep out the window and see two police officers. You become excited and open the door anticipating that good news awaits. Seeing the officers, you assume that I have been caught and your items will soon be returned. You open the door only to be informed that I had been contacted, but your items will remain in my possession because their superiors concluded that I had "extracted" the household items and "traded" for the car.

3. Chukwudieze, *Postcolonial African Philosophy,* 5.

The concept of stealing must transcend local laws formulated by us, because it is easy to write laws that will not classify the behavior we want to engage in as stealing. Put simply, if you take something that you know does not belong to you, you are stealing.

I think I can state with absolute certainty that had the scenario above happened, you would shout from the rooftops that you had been totally ripped off. That is because you knew that you had never given your consent to any of it. If I am right, then you may be on the road to understanding Bob Marley's sentiments when he sings about Africans being stolen. The people Mr. Marley sang about never experienced true freedom even when emancipated because they were not free to go "home" to Africa—and they were neither economically, nor legally, nor socially free if they remained.

Consider Sylvia Dubose, an African slave who fought her way to freedom in the South. She then traveled hundreds of miles north only to find herself still a member of the out-group. Geography and culture changed nothing. She obtained her freedom only to have her status challenged on sight by a white male upon arrival in New Brunswick, New Jersey. Many, many times legally free Africans were illegally re-enslaved. That may have occasionally happened because people believed that words on a pass or legal document could be forged. But I am sure there were many instances when this re-enslavement was simply a matter of permissible kidnapping. Ms. Dubose remembers:

> On my way a man called to me and asked, "whose nigger are you?"
> I replied, "I ain't no man's nigger I belong to God—I belong to
> no man." He said, "Where are ya going?" I replied, "That's none
> of your business—I'm free; I go where I please." He came toward
> me and I put down my young one and showed him my fists, and
> looked at him. He moseyed off telling me that he would have me
> arrested as soon as he could find the magistrate.[4]

Biased Lenses

To create racial categories is flat out crazy in the first place because there is absolutely no scientific basis for different racial groupings and we've known that for a while. By definition it robs those who are not born into the "preferred" category of a chance to be accepted as normal. William James Jennings noted a time when "it was not at all strange to hear Indians,

4. Larrison, *Sylvia Dubois*, 70.

Chinese, and Japanese referred to as Niggers."[5] So you see the idea of racial inferiority is malleable, it is not fixed, and it is not always based on skin hue. Nevertheless, in modern American society, a white person does not see themselves as a "racial" person but as an ordinary person, and one with an innate ability to be neutral in matters of race.

Because they are so confident that their reality is *the* reality, their intentions should never be questioned, even while they are turning a deaf ear to the people who were robbed of equal social standing. Many who hold that mind-set believe the effects of past racism ended the minute they were born. They truly believe that racism could not possibly exist in 1995, 2005, 2019. That perception leads to the conclusion that if black people would simply behave better, or try harder, their lives would be better. Listen to these "well researched" observations made by *New York Times* best-selling author Heather Mac Donald:

> If American blacks acted *en masse* like Asian Americans for ten years in all things relevant to economic success—if they had similar rates of school attendance, paying attention in class, doing their homework, and studying for exams, staying away from crime, persisting in a job, and avoiding out of wedlock childbearing—and we still saw differences in income, professional status, and incarceration rates, then it would be well justified to seek an explanation in unconscious bias.[6]

My response to Heather Mac Donald's hypothesis comes in a paraphrase of singer David Bowie's song "Rebel, Rebel": "How could you know?" Would you assume that a person that graduated from Yale University, and attended Cambridge University before graduating from Stanford Law School, would also have amassed enough urban street creds to know exactly how black people behave and why? I would argue that even the use of statistical analysis to reach an opinion about the way a percentage of black youth act and perform in a school setting would not explain the "why." I believe that the why question can be answered best by a person with firsthand knowledge about what black life is really like.

Even when a white person chooses to live in an urban environment, it can only provide entry-level awareness of the challenges black people face. That is because the other whites in powerful positions will treat them very differently than their black neighbors in areas such as business and

5. Jennings, *The Christian Imagination*, 32.
6. Mac Donald, *The Diversity Delusion*, 107.

employment. It might also be true that the quote above may sound a bit strident on first read—but I am inclined to believe that more whites hold a variation of that sentiment than would care to admit. That is because I have heard many people express a similar opinion only using softer language. Let us listen in on another perception of why minority scholastic achievement may lag behind that of whites, found in a book titled *Biased*:

> The number of intensely segregated schools—where less than 10 percent are white—has more than tripled the last thirty years according to research by the UCLA Civil Rights Project. The share of black students who attend racially isolated schools has increased by 11 percent. And while black and Latino students tend to be in schools with a substantial majority of poor children, white and Asian students typically attend middle-class schools. Segregation is reaching epidemic levels in the central cities of the nation's largest metropolitan areas. The states of New York, Illinois, and California are the top three worst for isolating black students in urban settings.[7]

Why is there still a very real need to point out that people whose histories differ may actually have different viewpoints about that history—and each of them can contain elements of truth? Many conservatives firmly believe America has one story and that all of its citizens are equal parts of it, and every controversial discussion is filtered through that lens. The mention of any historical facts that contradicts this somewhat limited view is rejected or worse resented by them. It is difficult to understand how smart, big-hearted white Christians are unwilling to accept that the founding mantra of freedom and justice for all, did not mean all, only a particular segment of all. That is just history. I attribute that myopia to spiritual blindness more than to a stubborn and evil unwillingness to acknowledge a truth that is right before their eyes. Yes, stealing is a matter of taking something from someone else—but as with the racial blindness just mentioned—stealing can also prevent a person from grasping something both materially and conceptually.

7. Eberhardt, *Biased*, 210.

Stolen Valor

The Miriam-Webster Dictionary states that the word *valor* stems from the Middle English word *valour*, meaning "worth or worthiness."[8] Its usage was in many ways similar to the way we use the word *race*, to describe a personal quality or characteristic. Races as fixed categories in America makes them closed fraternities. I cannot walk into the US Census office and identify as an Asian because I am perceived to not have the same personal characteristics as an Asian person. Because of that, a census employee would demand I check African American or refuse to designate. Even if I were to learn the Japanese language, dress similar to the way the people in Japan dress, I would be viewed as only "acting Japanese." The military is also a closed fraternity: you are either one of the insiders or you are not. Stolen valor happens when someone purchases a uniform to trick someone into believing they possess the same characteristics as a person who had served in the military—in this instance bravery. That person would be "acting like a soldier" in much the same way I would have been accused of acting Japanese. I selected "Stolen Valor" for this section's heading not because of the military connotations, but because of a parallel that exists between being black and being a soldier—that is Post Traumatic Stress Disorder (PTSD). When a person is robbed of recognition for who they are, there are always consequences.

Military personnel live and carry out their daily activities in a place where they are an ethnic minority, in places such as Iraq, Vietnam, Korea, and so forth. Is that not true about black and Native people as a whole? Please understand I am not drawing an equivalency between military service and being black. I am saying that when a person experiences trauma, whether in a combat zone or on a city street, that person is subject to residual negative after-effects from it. Psychologists and psychiatrists use a tool named *The Diagnostic and Statistical Manual of Mental Disorders* to make evaluations as to the presence of PTSD. The *DSM* only calls for a trauma of some sort to have occurred to make the diagnosis of PTSD. It could be killing someone, being in a car wreck, being beaten by a mob, being denied entrance to a business because of skin color. It could be being spat at and called a nigger from a passing car while walking in your neighborhood (happened to me), and a host of other triggers. Consider the actual portal for PTSD from some psychiatric literature I found online:

8. Dictionary.com, "Valor," para. 3.

Diagnosis of PTSD requires exposure to an event that involved the actual or possible threat of death, violence or serious injury. Your exposure can happen in one or more of these ways:

- Directly experiencing the traumatic event(s)
- Witnessing, in person, the traumatic event(s) as it occurred to others
- Learning that the traumatic event(s) occurred to a family member or close friend
- Experiencing repeated or extreme exposure to aversive details of the traumatic event(s)[9]

Let us take a moment to unpack each of these diagnostic criteria for PTSD and see if my parallel is valid. The first one is directly experiencing a trauma, which is a psychological response to a terrible event. Keep in mind that the triggering event need not be horrendous in nature, it just needs to be bad enough to have a negative impact on a person's emotions. Two examples come to mind. Once someone called me a "dirty nigger" in grade school. Another time, a white woman that was walking in front of my home began to run as soon as I said, "Good morning." If you are wondering, she did stop running about five houses down the street. I know that it is hard for some of you to understand, or believe, that there remains a significant number of people out there that find a black person's mere existence threatening, and that's without them having to do one thing.

Even after decades of similar reactions that my presence in white spaces brings, it still hurts each time. Some ask, why do you people keep bringing up this stuff? The short answer is because it keeps happening. Most people accept the fact that trauma brought on by a twenty-four–month tour of military duty would have lingering effects. Yet, there are those that firmly believe that trauma brought on by centuries of racial abuse should not have any lingering effect at all. How can that be? Next time you want to think "just get over it" when hearing a black person describe their pain—think about how you would not interrupt a white veteran describing his or her pain and say, "Just get over it!"

9. Ncbi.nlm.nih.gov, "DSM-5 Diagnostic Criteria for PTSD."

Stolen Dignity

Ron Highfield wrote, "The English word *dignity* still retains overtones of the Latin words *dignus* (worthy) or *dignitas* (merit or worth). Dignity like worth comes in degrees."[10] That understanding, if accurate, would suggest that some are worthier or more dignified than others—at least some can possess more inherent dignity than others. If that is true, then there exists a preset continuum of dignity that we all must accept as being just how things are and order our societies in such a way that covers up any inconsistency. In that scenario, those who are farther along the dignity continuum must volitionally grant those who are not as advanced the amount of dignity they see fit. That is the way we have done race in America since its inception. However, philosopher Robert Spaemann wrote, "The deliberate humiliation of the weaker person is just as undignified as cowering before a stronger one."[11] In my view that is a lose/lose. That is why I really appreciate Donna Hicks definition that says, "Dignity is an internal state of peace that comes with the recognition of the value and vulnerability of all living things."[12] Racism does not do that because it robs those at the bottom of their internal peace, and sometimes their external or physical peace too. Professor Spaemann offered this countervailing perspective, "Human dignity is inviolable to the extent that others cannot take it from you."[13] Now wouldn't that be nice!

Many anthropologists and sociologists believe that humans evolved to cooperate—we get along to survive. I am sure you have heard those theories in one form or other. But racial categories do not lead to cooperation but competition. Then all bets are off because in that world, only the strong survive. However, a drive to survive in a world not designed for you to succeed is not a practical remedy because no amount of determination lasts forever. The resistance will eventually wear you down. One of the adages from professional boxing says that repeated blows to the opponent's body is the best route to exposing the head so real damage can be done. That is because the painful punches to the ribs, stomach, and heart begin to add up. The boxer unconsciously drops the hands to protect himself without considering that he is exposing a more sensitive area in the process. What if

10. Highfield, *God, Freedom, and Human Dignity*, 96.
11. Spaemann, *Love and the Dignity of Human Life*, 30.
12. Hicks, *Dignity*, 1.
13. Spaemann, *Love and the Dignity of Human Life*, 30.

that were true of the collective body of black Americans? Years of continuous punches to the figurative body are bound to have an effect on the head or mental outlook of the population. How long should a group of people be expected to endure punch after punch and keep up a happy face or positive outlook? A boxer is allowed a time-out in between each round. During that time he can tell his trainers what the amount of damage being done to him is and how it is affecting him.

But it is rare for a time-out to happen when black people can openly share about the damage done to their figurative bodies. Black people are discouraged from telling their stories in white spaces if those stories make white listeners uncomfortable. I remember being at a Bible study one night when I casually made reference to something that most black people have experienced. The white host cut me off with a dismissive, "Oh not one of those stories again!" My real-life experiences made her uncomfortable, and believe me they make me uncomfortable too. The difference is that she can avoid those situations simply by choosing not to acknowledge them, but I will have to live through them without any choice in the matter.

The way a person views the world determines what subjects they will believe to be pertinent to their life. Said another way, human beings reveal what is truly important to them by what they pursue and also what makes them angry. We are called to do more than coexist, as the popular bumper sticker suggests. We are called to develop a genuine concern for the people outside of our present circle of friends no matter how wide that circle may be. Perhaps a commitment to live out the slogan that says, "don't love others the way you think you should love them, but the way that God loves them," would take some of the pressure off us trying to figure out how.

Restoring Hope

I once asked a guitarist what could I do to improve my guitar playing. I expected him to show me some scales, maybe finger exercises, or something else of a technical nature. Instead, the answer I received came in one word, "practice." I explained to him that I did not know what to practice and that was why I was seeking his assistance. He replied, "Practice anything." It took a while, but I did learn to appreciate his philosophy. We should not worry so much about what to do, or how to do something, we should make sure we are doing something. My friend Robert often says, "something is better than nothing" when speaking about exercise as a means to get in shape. The takeaway is if you want to play guitar better, practice anything. If you want to run a marathon, get up and run. The same should hold true for reaching out to people who experience racism almost every day of their lives. The obstacle to navigate is that most white people in America have not experienced racism in forty or fifty years (and usually never). But for most of my black friends, it has been forty days, sometimes even forty minutes, since the last incident. That is why it is important for even those who have not experienced it to do something, anything, every single day to fight racism.

The historical pattern for white/black reconciliation in America has been incremental and the slower the better for some. Even in the Christian church, there has always been an unstated caution that we shouldn't move too fast. In other words, when it comes to solving racial discord, we should not try any and everything to combat it. (Practice anything) We should not wake up one morning and begin to do something. (Get up and run) Our pattern has been that we wait until everyone is somewhat comfortable, then hold a meeting to discuss how we can one day address the very real racial tensions that exist. That won't do. Racial reconciliation must start the same day one recognizes the problem and makes up his or her mind to get involved. As with the examples from music and sports, just start fighting racism and the how-to, and the best way, will come later.

In the evangelical world where I am ordained as a minister there have been many attempts at racial reconciliation. Those efforts have typically consisted of a proclamation in the form of "we agree that we should all be sorry that racism happens." Then, the leaders take the platform and they pray over each other. That is followed by a few minutes of group singing and then the people are dismissed to return to the status quo. I know of one denomination that scheduled the racial reconciliation track for the day after their conference officially ended. That resulted in the vast majority of white pastors missing the session because they were on their way home to their respective churches. I mention this not to put them or anyone else down but to highlight what a low priority racial justice has been in many white evangelical churches. I suggest that what is needed at this point in time is a Christian version of *teshuva*, meaning a complete repentance, or a returning. There are five factors in *teshuva* (repentance), each of which can be a starting point for the entire process, meaning they need not happen in order:

However, almost all agree that repentance requires five elements: recognition of one's sins as sins (*hakarát, ha-chét'*), remorse (*charatá*), desisting from sin (*azivát, ha-chét'*), restitution where possible (*peira'ón*), and confession (*vidui*).[14]

When I came to faith I did so through a recovery program that utilized the twelve steps from Alcoholics Anonymous. Let us arrange the principles of *teshuva* in a way that each element corresponds to a comparable AA principle in order to find a method for applying them across cultural and religious borders.

1. Recognition of one's sins: "We *admitted* we were powerless over the besetting problem—that our lives had become unmanageable."

2. Remorse: "Made a list of all persons we had harmed, and became *willing* to make amends to them all."

3. Desisting from sin: "Continued to take personal inventory and when we were *wrong* promptly admitted it."

4. Restitution where possible: "Made direct *amends* to such people wherever possible, except when to do so would injure them or others."

5. Confession: "We're *entirely* ready to have God remove all these defects of character."

To repent means we must admit the wrongs of the past if the future is to be brighter. There is just no other way for it to happen. Yes, it is true that the present is independent of the past, but it is equally true that the present is a result of the past. There are many racial groups that have been harmed by the policies of the American government, and as Christians it is imperative that we not only acknowledge them, but make the effort to own up to the true historical record. We also need to be brutally honest with ourselves and ask whether or not we presently hold similar attitudes of those from the past. Then ask ourselves if it is possible that we could be giving tacit approval to some equally questionable governmental polices even now, both knowingly and unknowingly.

14. Blumenthal, "Spiraling Towards Repentance," line 3.

Time for Healing

It is not debatable that this seventh Commandment means we are not to take from another human being that which belongs to them. What we are not comfortable with is taking responsibility for the outcome of that behavior. President Obama got in big trouble with many Americans when he said "You didn't build that" during a 2012 campaign speech. What they heard, and what he meant, could have been very different. I do not know exactly what he meant, but I know what I heard. What I heard was, if people want to have pride in America's many accomplishments by nature of being a citizen, then they must be equally willing to be remorseful about the injustices that were done. Said another way, most big things do not happen as a result of a few—they happen through the contributions of the many. That is true about our collective greatness, and it is also true about our collective failing, of which racism is one.

Repentance for the sin of stealing requires restitution when possible. Just imagine that you own a brand new Corvette. One of your friends from church asks to borrow it for a week. The week turns into months. You learn he has taken it to Florida and parked it at his vacation rental there. He is arrested in the state in which you live but the car remains in Florida. You visit him in jail where he asks for forgiveness and you forgive him. Then you tell him that you want the car back. He says no. Exasperated, you ask why not. He says he has asked God to forgive him, you have forgiven him, and what is past is past, and so why should he give the car back. That is analogous to the way some have been unwilling to restore the rights and dignity that were taken from entire races of people.

If as a nation-state we are guilty of stealing a group of people's labor, land, dignity, sense of self, etc., we should acknowledge that fact. The second step from Alcoholics Anonymous indicates we need to be willing to return those items to them, and the fourth says to actually do it. The key words in the fourth step are "wherever possible." However, that last phrase is not a free pass to ignore the second because the steps close pointing us in the direction of an act of humility and contrition. The last step asks that we ask God to remove the very shortcomings in our personalities that would keep us from wanting to engage in a *teshuva* in its fullest application.

10

Narratives

You Shall Not Bear False
Witness against Your Neighbor (Exod 20:16).

KASH REGISTER IS REALLY a great name, is it not? It is not a pseudonym, but the real name of a real person. Sadly, and cool factor aside, that name is associated with a terrible miscarriage of justice that occurred in 1979. Kash Register was wrongly convicted of murdering a woman, and then after thirty-four years in prison, his conviction was overturned. He was released from prison when it came to light that he had been convicted on the false testimony of two witnesses. One of the people who assisted him in gaining his freedom was law professor Laurie Levenson. She said, "The only reason he was convicted was some witnesses lied and then the prosecution and police hid some valuable evidence."[1]

Recently a friend told me about an inmate who is on death row in Texas and is unable to get a new trial. He has had all of his appeals turned down even though new and possibly exculpatory evidence has surfaced. A *New York Times* op-ed piece notes one comment about this case by a District Court of Appeals judge that is relevant to our discussion. Judge Keith Ellison wrote in his opinion that, "Federal law does not recognize actual innocence as a mechanism to overturn an otherwise valid conviction."[2] Those two cases made this statistic sobering, "Mistaken eyewitness

1. Abc7ny.com."Wrongly Convicted Man Released," para. 8.
2. Grissom, "Appeal of Death Row Case," line 13.

identifications contributed to approximately 71% of the more than 360 wrongful convictions in the United States overturned by post-conviction DNA evidence."[3] It is difficult to be sure of the intent of a witness when their testimony consists of mistaken identification in a court of law. But we can surmise that when inaccurate eyewitness testimony is given, it is a short step to it being false testimony. Preventing travesties in court-related matters could be one of the reasons that songwriter Bob Dylan warned against "talking falsely" in one of his songs, because it can be so easy to do. That also illustrates one of the reasons why the ninth Commandment was given to Moses: to encourage us to be extremely careful about what it is we say about another person.

In most areas of life, truth telling is a prized commodity. However, there are occasions when it is difficult to be sure what truth actually is. Consider the classic liar's paradox that philosophers have wrestled with at least since the time of Plato. If a liar says to you that they are lying, they are telling the truth, but that creates a contradiction in terms, since if they are telling the truth, they would not be a liar. Confused? Me too, but the brain twist was needed to illustrate a point, and that is, "What is it that a person must do or say to be lying?" Are there situations when lying is not only appropriate, it is the right thing to do? Is telling an untruth the only definition for lying? Not really, because as the liar's paradox illustrates, people can and do tell lies without ever uttering words that are factually untrue, and vice versa.

Porkies and Wolf Tickets

America society accepts a host of narratives that would not pass the "absolute truth" sniff test. History has shown that these false narratives are often times the pathway to convincing an entire population of the righteousness of very bad ideas. We need look no farther than the eugenics movement, when people began to believe that a perfect society could be achieved scientifically. That thinking gave us Hitler. Then there is the fact that advertising firms make enormous sums of money using false narratives to manage perceptions so that the consumer will purchase items they do not really need. My point is that there are lies and then there are lies. Julaine and I are addicted to English detective mysteries. One detective named Inspector Frost calls the outright lies people use to deflect suspicion "porkies."

3. Innocenceproject.org. "Mistaken Identifications," line 1.

On the other hand, there was a famous rock musician who would often spin fantastic tales and then end them by saying, "wolf." That was a signal that he had just sold the listener a wolf ticket—a light-hearted fable. Selling wolf tickets was patterned after the boy in Aesop's fable who repeatedly cried wolf when there was not a wolf around. The boy would sound the alarm about an imaginary wolf so often that when a wolf did show up, he was not believed. Selling wolf tickets was not thought of as lying—it was just good clean fun. The two examples of lying so far are quite different from each other. In the first instance a lie is told to deceive, whereas in the second a lie is told to entertain.

When I lived in Los Angeles, I read the *Times* religiously. For some reason it never occurred to me that *my* news source could ever be biased. I believed the *LA Times* accurately reported on events that had occurred in places where I was not. I was certain that the paper's only agenda was to give spin-free information. It never entered my mind that they would try to control the way I would interpret the news they presented. It wasn't until I moved to Belize City that I came to understand that it is next to impossible for any news organization not to have a bias. Belize is a country just south of Mexico and east of Guatemala. It is a relatively small country but ethnically diverse. It was once a British colony—later a British protectorate—finally it was granted complete independence in 1981. The country's roots are English, and it has a parliamentarian form of governance with two political parties vying for power every election. Each party owns its own newspaper, and any story that is newsworthy gets reported by each party's paper. Naturally those stories are presented in a way that is consistent with that party's convictions.

Consider a hypothetical that illustrates how having each political party owning its own news agency plays out. Let us imagine it is 3 AM and we are at a local bar located on a busy street in the downtown area. A person decides to go to the restroom but is so drunk that he is unaware that he is actually walking out the front door. He walks about ten steps and boom, he is hit by a passing vehicle and killed. The next day one party's news headline reads, "Due to the failed policies of the previous government a man loses his life." The article suggests that the reason for the tragedy was an inadequate number of streetlights. As one might expect, the headline of the rival newspaper read quite differently: "The government's budget cuts on police funding has resulted in a death on our streets." Their article goes on to state that the prime minister has failed to provide adequate funding for the police, and so there are not enough officers patrolling the streets of our city. That failure by the government is what caused a man to lose his life. The actual facts of the story are that the man was so drunk that he proceeded into the street without taking proper precaution. When the aim is to advance a narrative, facts can be something that get in the way.

Hiding inside a Pea Bottle Narrative

Charles Maurice de Talleyrand said, "Speech was given to man to disguise his thoughts."[3] Withholding information is another popular method used by people that are not desirous of being truthful. In high school my best friend's name was Brad Gardner. Brad and I spent a lot of time at Circus Billiards in San Jose, California. His nickname, "Donut Brad," was given to him by the people at the pool hall. Brad worked at his father's Winchell's Donut franchise a block from the pool hall. One of the games played at the hall was officially named kelly pool, but in less formal settings it was called pea pool.

Blue Ball was an alcoholic and usually one social security check away from homelessness. Like most of the people that frequented Circus Billiards, Blue Ball enjoyed wagering on pool games. As with most gamblers, he won some and he lost some. His love of spirits also contributed to him being broke most of the time. Many regulars would not bet much money when they played him. Not because they were afraid of losing—they were afraid of winning and taking what little money he had away from him. Yes, everyone liked Blue Ball. He was a jovial and upbeat guy with tons of entertaining stories acquired by having lived in almost every state in America. No one ever knew which ones were true, but that did not matter, because Blue Ball was a storyteller and he told stories colorfully.

To set up how Blue Ball and the ninth Commandment intersect, allow me to give you a picture of the way pea pool was played. To start the game little round peas with numbers one to fifteen are placed in a small bottle. The bottle is then shaken and each player takes a numbered pea. The number on the pea taken by a player directly corresponds to the number on the ball that player must sink in order to win. Each player takes a turn shooting at the fifteen balls on the table in numerical order beginning with the one ball. They are allowed to continue shooting until they miss. Should a player sink someone else's ball before sinking theirs, the owner of the numbered ball that was pocketed must pay the shooter the dollar amount of the bet.

Since the peas were placed in a small dark bottle, the remaining peas are not visible. That means the players involved are on an honor system as to which pea is actually theirs.

There were many days that four or five of us would play pea pool just to pass the time and so it was not serious gambling. The stakes might be a quarter per "pea'd" ball and a dollar for the person who sank the most balls belonging to others during the game. Quite often when Blue Ball was involved in the game it could end without him ever divulging his number. He would choose not to speak up because if he remained silent, he wouldn't have to pay the player that had sunk his ball. Once it became obvious that he was cheating by withholding his number, someone would call him on it and ask, "Which ball did you have, Blue Ball?" He would sheepishly respond with a line that became somewhat famous, "Um, I don't know, I'd better check my pea!" Blue Ball's use of a feigned lack of certainty as to the actual number of his pea walked the thin line between being reticent and lacking candor. That is an activity that most of us must engage in daily. Is that violating the ninth Commandment?

Massaging a Narrative 'til It Fits

The stories we tell can elevate or destroy a person and often times we do both. Intentionally controlling people's impressions is one of the tools used to establish false narratives. I had a brilliant Native friend named Richard Twiss. He and I had a few conversations about the story that America tells itself about the treatment Native and African peoples received throughout its history. We contrasted the bad treatment each group had endured by playfully asking the other in almost game show fashion, "Who had it worse?" We used this abstraction to speculate that Christians of European descent could not be aware of the cruelties their forebears foisted on other human beings and celebrate the founding the way they do without any sense of guilt or shame. In fact, due to certain theological perspectives, some have characterized that unconscionable behavior as carrying out the will of God. We marveled at some of the false narratives used by the settlers and slave owners to justify their behavior. They were false, obtuse, and grounded in self-deceit. It is important that you fully understand this one thing. The fruit of those false narratives ended with Native Americans being treated like a conquered foe on their own homeland and with people of African descent being treated much like captured animals.

No amount of denial, revisionist verbiage, or massaging the narrative can expunge the American track record of immorality when it comes to race. One example of a revisionist narrative is found in a textbook my friend's son brought home. This book is in use in Texas schools and it portrays slavery as being a time when African people did work without being paid. Then there is the following narrative that a large number of white Christians accept. They argue that black people have experienced a hard time, but it was just a minor bump on the road to human progress. Then there is the narrative about Native people that portrayed *them* as having started the wars with the settlers. One American colloquialism that resulted from that perception can be seen in a term that I grew up with, "Indian giver." That was a derogatory name you would call someone if they wanted to take something back. That saying was the result of another myth about the West. That was the myth that the Indians gave the land to the settlers and then changed their mind. That myth was well established in the minds of many of my white playmates growing up, and it illustrates the power of narrative. Listen to what actor and American folk hero, John Wayne, said during an interview at that time.

> I don't feel we did wrong in taking this great country away from them, if that's what you're asking. Our so-called stealing of this country from them was just a matter of survival. There were great numbers of people who needed new land, and the Indians were selfishly trying to keep it for themselves.[4]

The narrative of the courageous settler was in full bloom in my formative years. John Wayne's movies were on television a lot when I was a young and impressionable boy. In many of those movies the problems between the Indians and the settlers usually centered around Native people not wanting to live on a reservation. Hence our adage for people who are out of place, meaning beyond the control of the Americans, is "off the reservation." People like John Wayne, both the actor and the citizen, rarely question why the Natives were forced onto reservations in the first place. I included Mr. Wayne's perspective not for the facts about the subject matter, but for his attitude about the subject matter. Many times, it is our attitudes that need adjustment to be open to more than one view about a historical fact. Mr. Wayne's perspective illustrates just how an organizing myth can be based on a totally false narrative from the beginning. Author Rene Girard offered

4. Rosenberg, "John Wayne," para. 11.

some insight into how these types of myths can also shield a society from accountability. He wrote, "Myths justify violence against the scapegoat, the community is never at fault."[5]

Contradictory Narratives

I recently taught a class at a seminary where I opened with the question "what is an ethnic group?" Then I asked, "What is a cultural group?" followed by "What is a racial group?" You'd be amazed at the responses I received. The answers the students put forward bled into each other and were inconsistent, to put it mildly. Their rationale for which group of people should be placed in what category was ahistorical and illogical. I left the class that day sad that there are people that live their lives every day believing that there are mysterious "others" out there for them to fear. Even when our opinions about others are couched in anthropological, sociological, or even nationalistic language, they are still perception-based and can be wrong. Even though many Christians recognize their perceptions may be wrong, they hold on tightly to the practice of "otherization" to the degree that maintaining a loving acceptance of people different from them is a major stretch. Once faulty narratives have become entrenched, they are difficult to dislodge no matter how weak or inconsistent they are.

Unlike African Americans, most foreign-born darker-skinned people have been granted a temporary exemption from racial stereotypes and the reflexive distrust that comes with having dark skin. However, it does not take long for them to take on the biases and prejudices of the majority without realizing it. People from those groups have never been feared or loathed the way African Americans have been throughout our history. These darker-skinned people from outside the US are not aware of our culture's nuanced racial attitudes. Many people in these nonwhite people-groups are blind to how racism operates, even when it happens right before their eyes. They often miss the subtle coded signals that are sent in public spaces.

Recently a close friend who is white was involved in a financial transaction where the first point of contact was a darker-skinned person from India. The interaction between the two was upbeat and cordial. However, when a second employee, an African American male with dreadlocks, surfaced to complete the transaction, my friend's demeanor changed dramatically. Rather than speaking to him the same way she had the first employee,

5. Girard and Merrill, *When These Things Begin,* 33.

she deferred to another colleague to complete the transaction. I am certain that the slight was unintentional because this person is a very close friend. However, due to the taboo against white women interacting with black males left over from the slavery era, she reacted in a way that would be "understandable" to many Americans. That story illustrates why, even after centuries of people attempting to undo the damage the country's founding narratives established, social interactions between black and white remain poor. We really are to love our neighbors, even when we think of them as strange for whatever reason. That will never happen until we have fact-checked many of the stories we have always accepted as true. Then those stories can be retold with the characters recast in such a way that new and more just narratives are created.

A Narrative of Welcome

Racial division continues in the social and political realm. It saddens me that even Christian people find it perfectly acceptable to harbor so many negative feelings about people of color. How can this still be happening in 2019? I gave one possible answer in one of my earlier books, and that is racial cognition. That is the practice where people "run every thought about, and impression of, another human being through a racially coated filter."[6] One of the core values of our faith community here in Austin is that we intentionally see the world spiritually rather than politically, racially, psychologically, or economically. That means what is spiritual should be the main lens utilized when viewing everything about life.

Racism is not spiritual and so it should follow that a spiritual person would not ever want to hold any view that is even remotely racist. If that logic holds, then our churches need to step up, acknowledge the reality of current racism, and become involved in the fight against it. The church's failure to model lifestyles that reflect the love of Christ only invites open-ended attacks about religion such as these by atheist author Christopher Hitchens, for whom religion is "violent, irrational, intolerant, allied to racism, and tribalism."[7] Pretty harsh, huh? However, if the church had been doing a better job of being the church, those words could never have been written. Is it possible that as a church, we have actually earned every one of those labels at one time or another? I think we have, and bringing ethics

6. Calhoun, *A Story of Rhythm and Grace*, 53.
7. Quoted in Long, *Christian Ethics*, 1.

back into the conversation in our churches each week is what will keep us from repeating them.

Many people find loving the stranger too impractical, and rather than challenge that notion and make an effort to do better, they rebrand kindness, being polite, and not intentionally harming someone as loving them. Contrast that with what George M. Lamsa said hospitality was like in Jesus' time: "In the East every family expects guests to enter without notice day or night. In countries where hotels and restaurants are unknown and where hospitality necessarily dominates, people believe that it is a sin to sell bread. Strangers and travelers are welcome." He then offers two quotes that clarify what welcome means: "A house without a guest is a house without a blessing" and "Today he is our guest; and some day we may be his."[8] Native people had much the same idea about the meaning of welcome. To share a tepee with someone was a given, even if that someone was a stranger. My Native friends have shared many stories indicating that their idea of hospitality was to honor their guests by giving them the most comfortable seating, allowing them to use their possessions as though they belonged to them, and serving them the best food. They said the latter would be true even at times when they were not sure that they would have food for the next day. There are times when being a community of welcome involves not being comfortable.

Narratives of Community

Communities of Fate

Churches tell themselves that they cannot help being homogeneous. One of the more common reasons that people give for why they attend a homogeneous church is that "the church is in my neighborhood." Another is, "I feel comfortable at this church." Yet another is, "I just feel called to this church and I cannot explain why." Notice that there is one underlying theme running through all three: I do not attend this church due to my preferences, but because of circumstances somewhat beyond my control. In the first, the fact that I live in a racially homogeneous community is why I attend this all-white church, and it is not my fault. The second reason is based on the idea that a church should be a place where a person feels comfortable. It's natural for people to be comfortable around others like themselves, so

8. Lamsa, *My Neighbor Jesus,* 60–61.

it is not anyone's fault that they attend an all-white church—besides, isn't everybody else doing the same thing? The last reason is the most powerful one: God called me here! A calling by God is what is responsible for their church selection, and who can argue against that?

Communities of Faith

Churches that are intentionally inclusive often embrace a Trinitarian concept of God. That being, Jesus, God the Father, and the Spirit are one. Perhaps the people who attend those churches are more open to seeing individuals from different people-groups becoming one, than churches that do not emphasize the Trinity. For that reason, an inclusive church sees it as simply a foregone conclusion that it is possible for its attenders to be one in Jesus. That is a special kind of unity. Churches grounded in that type of faithful communion aspire for the story of a three-in-one God to be their story. This type of community can only flourish when there exists an unshakeable faith in this verse, "For he himself is our peace, who has made the two groups one and has destroyed the barrier, the dividing wall of hostility."[9] If that verse is not fully embraced, all that will happen is people will create new types of barriers, or simply move the old barriers to new locations.

Communities of Love

These are churches that pursue mutuality and they see outsiders as future insiders at every level. There are many white churches that have people of color attending them each week. That is a good start, but that should not be the end. It is not enough to have lighter-skinned and darker-skinned people share a service and then return home to their respective neighborhoods. That is not "doing life together," that is enjoying a religious event together. Why should we call what happens in bars, football games, and other public spaces such as parks and schools, a picture of genuine Christian community? In each of those cases, people share a space for a set amount of time and then leave separately. A community of mutuality can only be actualized when people are willing to honestly confront the social segregation caused

9. Eph 2:14, NIV.

by the systems, structures, and narratives that contributed to a fractured world in the first place.

The narratives that are thrown our way by the media, and what we accept as being true about them, expose our biases. There have been many stories told about people of color that have shaped the way the majority culture views them. Then there are other stories that have caused the majority culture to believe what they do about themselves. It is possible that one or both of those witnesses are false. What I want you to take away from this chapter is this—remember they are just stories. Some stories are better than others, and some stories are truer than others. Some stories are told in better ways than others, and that can result in them being accepted without much scrutiny. A story told well is still a story, and that does not necessarily mean that it is actually true. However, there is one story that will always be true, and that is Jesus' story of love for us. Finally, that story is the only narrative that matters.

I I

Returning

**You Shall Not Covet Your Neighbor's House
or Anything Else That Belongs to Him (Exod 20:17).**

As we begin this final chapter, consider this statement: "The only thing contrary to God is self-will!"[1] The idea of "self-will" is what this Commandment addresses. In the introduction to this book the question was raised, "What is soul?" The answer I provided was that it is the intersection of the human and divine, the seat of our ethics and morals that are the nucleus of the good society. The writer of Psalm 19:7 says that the soul is revived by the Commandments that we have been discussing. As we close our conversation about the Ten Words, one question remains: what happens within the soul? We have discussed that the soul is the root of our moral and ethical tree, but how? God has given us the freedom of will to build on his moral code, and when we filter our desires through a satisfied soul, we are able to progress.

Our social evolution is not the result of luck, ingenuity, or instinct, as it happens in the animal kingdom. It is a result of the choices we make as a species. This is somewhat like the view of Buddhist Gelongma Karma Migme Chödrön: "All animals also are able to free themselves from the objects of enjoyment (*kāmaguṇa*). But they do not know how to cultivate

1. D'Sousza, *The Way of Jesus,* 111.

the good in view of the Path."[2] We humans do have guide rails to keep us morally grounded on our journey. Sociologists Christian Smith writes:

> Human animals are moral animals in that we possess a capacity and propensity unique among all animals: we not only have desires, beliefs and feelings (which often have strong moral qualities) but also the ability and disposition to form strong evaluations about our desires, beliefs, and feelings that hold the potential to transform themselves. Canadian philosopher Charles Taylor refers to us as having second order desires—desires about our desires.[3]

Desires are inherent to most species within the animal kingdom, and most engage in activities to satisfy them. Consider the words *desire*, *jealousy*, and *rivalry* in the context of coveting. Before we begin, read Professor Leonard Greenspoon's definition of coveting" "to desire (someone or something) obsessively, wrongfully, and/or without due regard for the rights/feelings of others."[4] Now consider James K. A. Smith on desires: "It's not what I think that shapes my life from the bottom up; it is what I desire."[5] Our desires can be the impetus for the decisions made in life. Let us take a look at three ways that wrong desires can sometimes lead us to ruin.

The Basics

Coveting as Desire—I Want, I Want, I Want

I once toured with a nationally known musician who allowed his selfish desire to take over his personality. That lack of discipline eventually led to the ruin of the name that he had worked hard to make famous. When a band tours, there are people at every stop offering a variety of "goodies" in order to ingratiate themselves with the band members. Remember the groupies from a previous chapter? The people I am speaking about had much the same mind-set because their main goal was to please the band. My colleague had a knack for attracting people like this and then mesmerizing them with his larger-than-life persona. Once he had gained their confidence, he would extract everything he could from them in terms of drugs, favors, and even money. He once stole a guitar from one of the

2. Gelongma, "Maha Prajnaparamita," para. 8.
3. Smith, *Moral Believing Animals*, 8–9.
4. Greenspoon, "Do Not Covet," para. 5.
5. Smith, *Desiring the Kingdom*, 51.

band members and sold it. Another time he walked into a clothing store and expected the proprietor to give him the clothing on the strength of his name, and an altercation ensued. As his desire for more, more, and more took root—his antisocial tendencies grew and grew. Eventually, he became involved in behavior that could only be described as out of control, which led to a couple of stints in prison.

Toward the end of his career he had abandoned all pretense of having any respect for the people around him. He just flat out used them. There was one instance when someone came to a performance driving a Corvette. My ex-bandmate "borrowed" the car and then drove it to another state. His greed-filled desires reached the point to where he would simply walk up to someone and ask, "Can I have that?" As difficult as it might be to imagine, there were many times when people would enthusiastically acquiesce to his outlandish requests. Unchecked desire can consume a person because once desire has crossed over to greed, the desire becomes insatiable and always in need of a new object on which to fix its gaze. The story ends with my friend losing everything materially, including the respect and adulation his talent had deservedly earned him.

Please do not miss the point of the previous example just because it was in the world of rock and roll, and we all know what happens to those types of people. I have witnessed the same attitude in churches, with much the same outcomes. The root is selfish desire, and we are all capable of falling into that trap, and that is why the tenth commandment was given. It wasn't given to straighten "them" out, it was given to prevent *us* from embracing the temptations that come to us all. I have seen clergy who were so obsessed with success that they behaved much like my rock and roll colleague. I cannot say with certainty that the clergy were doing anything improper, but I have seen a few "strong leaders" in the church appear to use people in ways that were at least questionable. Desires are desires, regardless of how we characterize them. Uncontrolled desire results in the chant, *I want, I want, I want.* That is a trap, and the question is, how do we avoid that trap? I suggest that we martyr, rather than kill, such desires. Killing is an act of violence, while martyrdom is an act of selflessly letting go. People will have a tough time trying to "kill" every illicit desire. That does not mean they have to give in to them, or that they can't let go of them.

Coveting as Jealousy—What about Me?

Michael Lewis has written that jealousy begins at the "latter half of the second year of life along with embarrassment and empathy."[6] I am going to go out on a limb and suggest that envy and jealousy are more closely related than envy and rivalry. I am not basing this on the result of an etymological survey of the possible meanings for each word, only my usage of them. I am characterizing the feeling of being jealous as analogous to that of a perceived lack. You know, that empty feeling we sometimes have when something long desired is just out of reach, therefore impossible to attain. Then, something strange happens. Some other person gets what you believed you deserved. At that point the desire becomes more intense, doesn't it? You want what has been the object of your desire even more. At the final stage, the fixation changes from being about what it is, to who has it. That is jealousy, and it may have more in common with insecurity than pride.

Sly Stone is a Rock and Roll Hall of Fame musician who at one stage of his career was the number one black entertainer in the world. He and I grew up in the San Francisco Bay area around the same time. Prior to his ascension to international superstardom, he and I had traveled in much the same circles, knowing many of the same people. When Sly and the Family Stone performed at Woodstock to rave reviews, I was elated. I saw their success as my hometown crew making the big time. However, many of our mutual friends were upset with their success, and with Sly in particular. Their thinking went something like this. "Oh, now Sly is big time, huh? He thinks he is too good to frequent the old nightspots on Broadway where he used to sit in with various bands." The band's success caused some of us to believe we could follow in their footsteps. While others seemed to respond with an attitude that said, "I will never have what they have and so life's not fair."

Their negativity was about them not having what someone else had, even though they started as friends. Sly and the Family Stone was a better band than the one I was in at the time. But our band, Leon's Creation, became a better band because of them. In this instance, jealousy did not lead to coveting, it inspired. In the other scenario jealously led to coveting. That covetous mind-set led to artistic paralysis that found its resolution in bitterness and resentment, which added together epitomizes jealousy.

6. Lewis, "Emotions," para. 3, line 7.

Coveting as Rivalry: The Drive to Succeed

Legendary college basketball coach John Wooden wrote, "Success is peace of mind, which is a direct result of self-satisfaction in knowing you made the best effort you are capable of making."[7] In my view that is a wonderful maxim. However, it raises one immediate question—how does anyone know what qualifies as their best effort? Consider the following hypothetical. The day basketball star LeBron James was born—his identical twin brother was stolen from the hospital. His mom decided not to tell LeBron or anyone in his family about the facts surrounding his birth, thinking it would not be of any benefit to them. Shortly after leaving the hospital the brother was spirited away to the coast of Senegal. All through his childhood, the brother lived in an isolated village far removed from television, and any other form of contact with the world outside. Eventually a mission team from America came to his village. They brought a basketball and a hoop with them, then left them when they returned home.

LeBron's brother loved the basketball and hoop and spent countless hours playing with it. In fact, he spent the same amount of time his unknown twin was spending thousands of miles away in Akron, Ohio. Then a miracle happened, LeBron found out about his brother and sent for him. Upon arriving at LeBron's mansion, the brothers found themselves in the gym playing basketball. Once they begin playing, it was evident that LeBron's brother was as bad at basketball as LeBron was great. How could that happen when the two shared identical genetic make-up? Besides, they invested the same amount of time practicing each day—and they each strived to be the best they could be. Why the disparity in outcome? Perhaps philosopher Rene Girard can help us here.

Girard developed the idea of mimetic desire, in which every human being is innately inclined towards imitation and jealousy. Michel Treguer described the effect that inclination can have this way: "We each desire what the other desires," with the result of "inexorable competition."[8] The person you admire for who they are or what they have, becomes your enemy for those same reasons. What we get are competition, jealousy, and imitation. It has been said by many that competition brings out the best in us. Jealousy, in this context, could be a motivator more so than the way I described it in the previous section. Imitation could also be a tool for a person to use

7. Wooden, *Wooden's Pyramid*, 14.
8. Girard and Merrill, *When These Things Begin*, 1.

in developing their skill. You see, in the hypothetical involving LeBron's twin, I believe it was not having access to television to see other players to imitate, and not having his brother around with whom to compete, that caused him to be a lousy player. The word that pushes this type of rivalry into the negative column is *jealousy*. Let those ahead of you inspire you rather than frustrate you. Your time will come.

The Desires Within

Three emotions comprise coveting: desire, jealousy, and rivalry. These desires are formed in the heart. The mind and body are but the method of delivery for those desires—and they influence our lives way beyond our emotions. One way to counter-balance this is to examine the word choices we make that can mask what resides in our hearts. There are times when we are unaware that our actions are singing a different song than the one we verbally broadcast. For example, a person can say "I am not racist," when all of their friends know that they are uncomfortable around darker-skinned people—they refuse to set foot in black neighborhoods—and rarely have a positive reaction to any news story about them. What speaks loudest? Making room in your heart for the other requires that you think outside of yourself. Thinking beyond the self is not accomplished by believing the right things or even acting in a certain manner. It is accomplished via a soul that longs to follow in the way of Jesus. Jesus made room in his heart for others, even while he hung on a cross dying.

At one point in his life King David allowed his heart to be polluted by selfish desires, jealousy, and rivalry. He knew what was needed for him to overcome his bent towards covetousness and asked God to "create in me a pure heart."[9] For the sake of discussion, let us define the word *pure* here to mean new, rather than spotless or perfect. David's covetous behavior began with him seeing a beautiful woman and desiring her. If as in David's case, covetousness could be a correlate to a visual appetite, then it could be overcome through a diet. But a diet is a means of controlling or curbing one's appetite for something, and not transforming the heart to desire something different. David was wise to ask God for a new, unblemished, and uncorrupted heart (soul). That is because the antidote for coveting is learning to see life in a completely different way—with a new set of desires for the heart to long for.

9. Ps 51:10, NIV.

The Kind of Love That Satisfies the Soul

I write this final section having just learned that one of my heroes and distant colleagues, Jean Vanier, has just entered into his heavenly peace. Mr. Vanier was the founder of L'Arche and a true hero for humanity. I did not have the privilege of meeting him, but I did see him as a colleague. That is because we both shared an unwavering commitment to befriend people society calls disabled, but I call differently abled. It was in the differently abled community that I learned what it means to care for a person's soul. My friend and ministry partner Robert Watson-Hemphill and I visit their workshops, also known as day-habs, to play guitars with them. Many of the people we care for are unable to speak, and that makes it hard to know what they need. We visit, sing songs, pray for them while we sing, and then connect through the eyes to tell them we love them. One rehabilitation center we visit serves people that are non-hearing, and that leaves connecting through the soul as the only communication option. Consider a brief description of L'Arche:

> L'Arche communities in the United States provide homes and workplaces where people with and without intellectual disabilities live and work together as peers; create inclusive communities of faith and friendship; and transform society through relationships that cross social boundaries.[10]

Allow me to introduce you to the friend that ushered me into the world of the differently abled. I met Samantha Garen Lawrence in 2009 or 10. It is my understanding that Sammie was born "normal" until a neurological disorder resulted in her losing brain function. The physical challenges that resulted from her illness included speech difficulties, loss of control of some of her limbs, and hindered cognitive ability. Yet all through her preteen years Samantha exhibited a gift for music. She could play songs on the piano after only hearing them once. Unfortunately, Sammie's health continued to deteriorate, and we lost my friend two years ago. Her courage and her spirit live on. And although she was classified as intellectually deficient, I was able to learn a lot from her.

One of the life lessons Sammie taught me was how to gracefully handle vulnerability. By that, I mean accepting who you are, how you are, and your limitations—then living with them rather than attempting to overcompensate for them. She did not choose the circumstances that resulted in her

---

10. Larcheusa.org, "Who We Are," para. 2.

being classified "special needs." She was special, but she had no more needs than the next person, just different needs. Samantha would get frustrated, not with life, but with how people treated her. Her bigger frustrations would surface when she saw somebody involved in an activity that she had been able to do at one time. But she even handled those disappointments with a gracious acceptance. Acceptance is one antidote to coveting because there is a power that acceptance brings that is not that obvious. The limited number of options available to Sammie gave her the opportunity to find contentment in ways that I certainly did not have the ability to see.

Sammie also helped me see that we are all vulnerable to some extent, only in different ways. Many of us expend an enormous amount of energy trying to inoculate, insulate, or develop shields that will protect us from the exposure that comes with vulnerability. Perhaps that is the hidden allure of coveting. That illusory component of coveting lies to us by telling us that whatever someone else has will do the trick. This is a different lie than the one that says if I just had that I would be happy. This lie tells us if we just had what they had, then we would not feel any more emptiness or pain. We convince ourselves that we can chart our own course, independent of anyone, including God. One interesting note is this. A few years ago, there was a saying in many Christian circles that said, "where God guides, God provides." But it was most often quoted as a lament when people were not satisfied with what they already had.

Meet Izabella the dancer. Izabella lives with an intellectual disability resulting from Down Syndrome. She has limited cognitive abilities but makes the most of what she has. She loves music, and has an acute sense of rhythm that manifests itself in a remarkable ability to dance. She also has a huge heart that results in her having a unique gift of empathic listening. One day, Samantha was in trouble with someone and was visibly upset when we arrived. Izabella sensed Sam's state of mind and reacted to it. She became distant from us, thinking we were the cause, and then shut us out completely. It required a few more visits to win back her trust. Today, she becomes excited when we enter, and usually says "I love you" to both me and my guitar. The point is, she is very aware of her surroundings, her friends, and proper interpersonal behavior, and she is content. Envy, jealousy, rivalry, and the hatred for "the other" are a part of our world—but they are not part of hers.

Meet Brian the singer. Brian is the first person that Samantha introduced me to at her rehabilitation workshop. He appears to suffer from severe brain and nerve damage, because his disability affects both his motor skills and his cognitive ability. He is rarely in a bad mood. He loves music, and he is always ready to join us for a good sing-a-long. He is unable to communicate via conversation, but he has a large repertoire of song lyrics committed to memory. He may be deficient in one area, but he is highly skilled in another. That is true about all of us, and that is why coveting the skills of someone else is such a waste of time. Brian cannot tell you the day of the week or what city he lives in, but he can ask for a hug and tell you that he loves you, and that is enough! There really is nothing more valuable in life than being loved and giving love. I believe that is true, and I also know the tendency to covet is always just a thought away. A pure desire is something that I must struggle to pursue, but it comes naturally to Brian. Who is the more abled?

The Heart's Desires

The purity of desire does not refer to right, correct, or even best, but the heart's desires. "Blessed are the pure in heart for they shall see God." Stripped down, this verse says that an uncluttered heart can see God, and I would add that an unbiased heart can see the world around it as it really is. The early church father St. Jerome said, "Plato located the soul in the head; Christ located it in the heart." It is the heart that reveals the actual substance of our desires. When we seek to alter what we pursue in life, it requires a change of heart more so than a change of will. Consider this prayer from antiquity:

> I adjure you, Puta, prince of forgetfulness, to remove stupid heart
> ... serious illness and all the worries and bad diseases and bloom-
> ing spirits and harming demons ... And give me an understanding
> heart, a heart that preserves what I hear and learn, and everything
> I learn I will not forget.[11]

It was Jesus who said that "the mouth speaks what the heart is full of."[12] If you listen to what a person talks about the most, you will know what is really important to them. I am not talking about the times they are choosing their words, or when they are "on," like at work—but casual conversation. What is your desire at this moment? Where will that desire

11. David, *Jurisprudence and Theology*, 120.
12. Luke 6:45, NLT.

take you today, this month, this year? Jesus' desire was for the kingdom of God to be realized. The kingdom of God is both a place and a state of being, where the love of God is enjoyed by all and is shared by all. James K. A. Smith states, "We are primordially and essentially agents of love, which takes the structures of desire or longing."[13] Our problem as a species is this: coveting pollutes our desires and turns inside the love that should be moving outside of us.

The root cause of coveting is best illustrated in a song I wrote several years ago. I wrote the song in response to The Rolling Stones' "I Can't Get No Satisfaction," and it contained the line "I ain't gonna quit till I'm satisfied." You can read into that line any meaning you like, but all I was doing was explaining why I was obsessed with practicing bass guitar. You see, I did not think I was a very good bass player. Even when notable musicians such as pianist Vince Guaraldi, bassist Ray Brown, and guitarist Jimi Hendrix would tell me that I had a gift, I didn't see it. The encouragement was good, but not seeing it myself was a problem. When a person is dissatisfied with himself or herself, dissatisfaction becomes a part of them. You don't control it, it controls you. Dissatisfaction in life can be the result of overly comparing ourselves to others. That can lead to being covetous of them. When that happens, we turn to manipulation to get what we covet from them, or of them. From that point on every word, smile, or action becomes calculated to achieve our ends, and like a drug, that can become an addiction.

The Apostle Paul says it requires intentionality to overcome habitual discontent. I lacked that at certain times and so does the average person who covets. As a high schooler, I would voice a desire to my parents for material things beyond our financial means. I would get the "true happiness does not come from getting the material things you want, but being content with what you have" speech. I usually received that speech this way: "You either think I am stupid, or you believe any old pacifier will calm me down, just like the ones you used when I was younger." I did not learn that it truly was within my power to be content in any, and every, situation until I began to have relationships with the differently-abled. It was not only the love I received from them that taught me about selfless love, it was observing how they loved each other.

Those are my friends, and in what some might see as a paradox, it is the people who have the least that have taught me the most. I have grown to love the differently-abled as they are, and because of that, I have learned

13. Smith, *Desiring the Kingdom*, 50.

to love me for who I am. It is in that space of letting go of what I once believed about myself, that I could begin the journey in the direction of the deep and lasting contentment best described as being soul-satisfied. This book opened with my asking that you "listen here," and I am closing it with another request that you "listen there." What does that mean? I ask that you listen, meaning pay attention to everybody you meet, and then listen to them with love.

Bibliography

Abc7ny.com. "Wrongly Convicted Man Released after 34 Years." https://abc7ny.com/archive/9319203.

Abelard, Peter. *Ethical Writings.* Indianapolis: Hackett, 1995.

Adamsmith.org. "The Theory of Moral Sentiments." https://www.adamsmith.org/the-theory-of-moral-sentiments.

Ali/Terrell. https://www.youtube.com/watch?v=-TJbjS2mdJE&t=77s.

Augustine. *Confessions.* Translated by Henry Chadwick. Oxford: Oxford University Press, 1998.

Axe, Douglas. *Undeniable.* New York: Harper One, 2016.

Balko, Radley. *Rise of the Warrior Cop: The Militarization of America's Police Forces.* New York: Public Affairs, 2014.

Bediako, Kwame. *Theology and Identity.* Bletchley, Milton Keynes, UK: Regnum, 1992.

Begbie, Jeremy S. *Theology, Music, and Time.* Cambridge: Cambridge University Press, 2000.

Bentley, Andrew. "Alcohol: It's Different for Native Americans." http://blog.nativepartnership.org/alcohol-its-different-for-native-americans.

Bergman, Jerry. *The Darwin Effect.* Green Forest, AR: Master, 2018.

Bibleodessey.org. "Was Moses' Name Egyptian?" https://www.bibleodyssey.org/en/people/related-articles/was-moses-name-egyptian.

Blumenthal, David J. "Spiraling Towards Repentance." https://www.myjewishlearning.com/article/spiraling-towards-repentance.

Bobonich, Christopher. *The Cambridge Companion to Ancient Ethics.* Cambridge: Cambridge University Press, 2017.

Boehm, Christopher. *Moral Origins.* New York: Basic, 2012.

Bornstein, Daniel E. *Medieval Christianity.* Minneapolis: Fortress, 2009.

Braineyquote.com. "Thoreau." https://www.brainyquote.com/search_results?q=thoreau.

Brock, Brian, and John Swinton. *Disability in the Christian Tradition.* Grand Rapids: Eerdmans, 2012.

Buber, Martin. *On Judaism.* New York: Schocken, 1967.

———. *Eclipse of God.* New York: Humanity, 1996.

Busvine, Douglas. "Collective Consciousness to Replace God (Dan Brown)." https://www.reuters.com/article/us-germany-bookfair-dan-brown/collective-consciousness-to-replace-god-author-dan-brown-idUSKBN1CH1O1.

Cahill, Thomas. *The Gift of the Jews.* New York: Anchor, 1999

Calhoun, Jimi. *A Story of Rhythm and Grace.* Eugene, OR: Cascade, 2018.

Cartwright, Dr. *DeBow's Review*. "Diseases and Peculiarities of the Negro Race: Dysaethesia Aethiopica." http://www.pbs.org/wgbh/aia/part4/4h3106t.html.

Chou, Vivian. "How Science and Genetics are Reshaping the Race Debate of the 21st Century." http://sitn.hms.harvard.edu/flash/2017/science-genetics-reshaping-race-debate-21st-century.

Chukwudieze, Emmanuel. *Postcolonial African Philosophy: A Critical Reader*. Cambridge, MA: Blackwell, 1997.

Clarke, John Henrik. *Christopher Columbus and the Afrikan Holocaust*. Buffalo, NY: Enworld, 1993.

Collins, John C., and Daniel C. Harlow. *Early Judaism*. Grand Rapids: Eerdmans, 2012.

Cowen, S. Marc. "Aristotle on the Soul." https://faculty.washington.edu/smcohen/320/psyche.htm.

———. "Aristotle on the Soul." https://faculty.washington.edu/smcohen/433/PsycheDisplay.pdf.

Crime Watch Daily. https://www.youtube.com/watch?v=RLxYxzPoqX8.

David, Joseph E. *Jurisprudence and Theology in Late and Ancient Medieval Jewish Thought*. New York: Springer, 2014.

Davidson, William. "Talmud (Shabbat 88b)." https://www.sefaria.org/Shabbat.88b?lang=bi.

Derrida, Jacques. *Acts of Religion*. 1st ed. New York: Routledge, 2001.

Dictionary.com. "Valor." https://www.dictionary.com/browse/valor.

Dictionary.cambridge.com. "Sound." https://dictionary.cambridge.org/us/dictionary/english/sound

Dickson, Athol. *Gospel of Moses*. Grand Rapids: Brazos, 2003.

Dijkstra, Jorrit R. "The Strength of Saharawi Women." https://thisisafrica.me/strength-sahawari-women.

Doumbia, Adam and Naomi. *The Way of the Elders: West African Spirituality & Tradition*. Woodbury, MN: Llewellyn, 2004.

D'Sousza, Tony. *The Way of Jesus*. Grand Rapids: Eerdmans, 2004.

Dunbar-Ortiz, Roxanne. *An Indigenous People's History of The United States*. Boston: Beacon, 2014.

Eberhardt, Jennifer L. *Biased: Uncovering the Hidden Prejudice That Shapes What We See, Think, and Do*. New York: Viking, 2019.

Encyclopedia.com. "Sounding." https://www.encyclopedia.com/social-sciences-and-law/political-science-and-government/military-affairs-nonnaval/sounding.

Exactlywhatistime.com. "Ancient Philosophy (Mythology)." http://www.exactlywhatistime.com/philosophy-of-time/ancient-philosophy.

Fackenheim, Emil L. *To Mend the World*. Bloomington, IN: Indiana University Press, 1994.

Famoustexans.com. "John Wesley Hardin." http://www.famoustexans.com/johnwesleyhardin.htm.

Farmer, Paul. *Pathologies of Power*. Berkeley, CA: University of California Press, 2005.

Fox, John. *Poetic Medicine*. New York: Tarcher Putnam, 1997.

Gelongma, Karma. "Maha Prajnaparamita Sastra." https://www.wisdomlib.org/buddhism/book/maha-prajnaparamita-sastra/d/doc225631.html.

Girard, Rene, and Trevor Cribben Merrill. *When These Things Begin*. East Lansing, MI: Michigan State University Press, 2014.

Glanton, Dahleen. "Red Onion." http://articles.latimes.com/1988-09-03/local/me-3081_1_red-onion-restaurant.

Bibliography

Goldstein, Shana. "On Hearing and Listening." https://reformjudaism.org/learning/torah-study/haazinu/hearing-and-listening.

Goldtooth, Dallas. "Dakota Man Exposes Vile History of Redskins." https://newsmaven.io/indiancountrytoday/archive/dakota-man-exposes-vile-history-of-redskins-tNKoJ1kxGkOao8FaHk4a7w.

Goodreads.com. "Marcus Aurelius." https://www.goodreads.com/quotes/7133477-if-anyone-can-refute-me-show-me-i-m-making-a-mistake.

Greenspoon, Leonard. "Do Not Covet." https://thetorah.com/do-not-covet-is-it-a-feeling-or-an-action.

Grissom, Brandi. "Appeal of Death Row Case More than a Matter Of Guilt or Innocence." https://www.nytimes.com/2012/03/11/us/texas-death-row-appeal-is-more-than-a-matter-of-innocence.html.

Haeckel, Ernst Sr. *The History of Creation vol. ii.* Boston: D. Appleton and Company, 1906.

Heschel, Abraham J. *The Prophets.* New York: Harper Perennial Classics, 2001.

Hicks, Donna. *Dignity: Its Essential Role in Resolving Conflict.* New Haven, CT: Yale University Press, 2011.

Highfield, Ron. *God, Freedom, and Human Dignity.* Downers Grove, IL: InterVarsity, 2013.

Hitler Meme. https://me.me/i/we-are-the-master-race-adolf-hitler-we-are-godes-1050 7117.

Horne, Gerald. *The Counter Revolution of 1776.* New York: New York University Press, 2014.

Iep.utm.edu. "God and Time." https://www.iep.utm.edu/god-time.

Ihs.gov. "Indian Health Services (Disparities)." https://www.ihs.gov/newsroom/factsheets/disparities.

Innocenceproject.org. "Mistaken Identifications are the Leading Factor in Wrongful Convictions." https://www.innocenceproject.org/eyewitness-identification-reform.

Jennings, William James. *The Christian Imagination: Theology and Origins of Race.* New Haven, CT: Yale University Press, 2011.

Jewfaq.org. "The Name of G-d." http://www.jewfaq.org/name.htm

Johnson, Carolyn Y. "Growing Brain Cells." https://www.independent.co.uk/news/science/minibrain-human-brain-cells-science-ethical-research-university-of-pennsylvania-a8521091.html.

Jones, Jacqueline. *A Dreadful Deceit.* New York: Basic, 2015.

Kahn, Alexander. "The Land of the Free and the Home of the Cool." https://www.claremont.org/crb/basicpage/the-land-of-the-free-and-the-home-of-the-cool.

Kalderon, Mark Eli. *Form without Matter: Empedocles and Aristotle on Color Perception.* Oxford: Oxford University Press, 2015.

Katzew, Ilona. *Casta Paintings: Images of Race in Eighteenth Century Mexico.* New Haven, CT: Yale University Press, 2015.

Larcheusa.org. "Who We Are." https://www.larcheusa.org/who-we-are.

Lamsa, George M. *My Neighbor Jesus.* Public Domain, 1932.

Larrison, C. W. *Sylvia Dubois: A Biography.* Oxford: Oxford University Press, 1988.

Lett, Woullard. "Readers Respond: Which Racial Terms Make You Cringe?" https://www.nytimes.com/2017/04/02/us/racial-terms-that-make-you-cringe.html.

Lewis, Michael. "Emotions." http://www.child-encyclopedia.com/emotions/according-experts/self-conscious-emotions.

Lexico.com. "Listen." https://www.lexico.com/en/definition/listen.

————. "Rely." https://www.lexico.com/en/definition/rely.

————. "Thief." https://www.lexico.com/en/definition/thief.

Long, D. Stephen. *Christian Ethics: A Very Short Introduction*. Oxford: Oxford University Press, 2010.

Lopez, German. "East Pittsburgh police officer charged for shooting." https://www.vox.com/identities/2018/6/20/17484480/antwon-rose-east-pittsburgh-police-shooting-video.

Lopez, Ian. *White by Law*. New York: New York University Press, 2006.

Mac Donald, Heather. *The Diversity Delusion*. New York: St. Martin's, 2018

Macmilliandictionary.com/. "Listen." https://www.macmillandictionary.com/us/dictionary/american/listen_1.

Marcus Aurelius. https://www.goodreads.com/quotes/7133477-if-anyone-can-refute-me-show-me-i-m-making-a-mistake2019marks.

McClendon, James. *Ethics: Systematic Theology*. Nashville: Abingdon, 2002.

McFarland, Ken. "Sunday Laws in America." http://libertymagazine.org/article/sunday-laws-in-america.

McGowan, Andrew B. *Ancient Christian Worship*. Grand Rapids: Baker Academic, 2014.

McTaggart, Lynne. *The Bond*. New York: Free, 2011.

Merkle, John. *Approaching God: The Way of Abraham Joshua Heschel*. Collegeville, MN: Liturgical, 2009.

Metzger, Paul Louis. "Driving While Black." Blog Interview with Jimi Calhoun. http://www.patheos.com/blogs/uncommongodcommongood/2017/06/driving-while-black.

Metzger, Paul Louis, and John W. Morehead. "What's the Big Deal about the Mormon Name Change?" http://www.patheos.com/blogs/uncommongodcommongood/2018/08/whats-the-big-deal-about-the-mormon-name-change.

Myjewishlearning.com. "Adultery." https://www.myjewishlearning.com/article/adultery/.

————. "Shabbat 101." https://www.myjewishlearning.com/article/shabbat-101.

————. "Teshuvah." https://www.myjewishlearning.com/article/spiraling-towards-repentance.

Ncbi.nim.nih.gov. "DSM-5 Diagnostic Criteria for PTSD." https://www.ncbi.nlm.nih.gov/books/NBK207191/box/part1_ch3.box16/?report=objectonly.

Nicholson, Graeme. *Justifying Our Existence*. Toronto: University of Toronto Press, 2009.

Niebuhr, Reinhold. *The Nature and Destiny of Man Volume II*. Lexington, KY: Westminster John Knox, 1943.

Noble, Denis. *Music of Life: Biology Beyond Our Genes*. Oxford: Oxford University Press, 2009.

Oden, Thomas C. *How Africa Shaped the Christian Mind*. Downers Grove, IL: InterVarsity, 2007.

Oxforddictionaries.com. "Ally." https://en.oxforddictionaries.com/definition/ally/.

————. "Beauty." https://en.oxforddictionaries.com/definition/us/beauty/.

Oz, Amos, and Fania Salzberger. *jews and words*. New Haven, CT: Yale University Press, 2012.

Parfit, Derek. *Reasons and Persons*. Oxford: Oxford University Press, 1984.

Prb.org. "Racial and Ethnic Differences in Mortality." https://www.prb.org/racialandethnicdifferencesinusmortality.

Pbs.org. "Africa American Women." https://www.pbs.org/wgbh/aia/part4/4p2956.html.

————. "Antebellum Slavery." https://www.pbs.org/wgbh/aia/part4/4p2956.html.

Pfaff, Donald J. *The Altruistic Brain: How We are Naturally Good.* 1st ed. Oxford: Oxford University Press, 2015.

Powell, John A. "Whiteness and Spatial Racism." https://racism.org/index.php/articles/race/white-privilege/397-whiteness15a/.

Quinn, Dave. "George Foreman." https://people.com/sports/george-foreman-10-kids-why-named-his-sons-george.

Reinhart, A. Kevin. *Before Revelation: The Boundaries of Muslim Moral Thought.* Albany, NY: State of New York University Press, 1995.

Reynolds, Thomas E. *Vulnerable Communion: A Theology of Disability.* Grand Rapids: Brazos, 2008

Richards, Keith. *Life.* New York: Bay Back, 2012.

Rodriguez, Gregory. "Roots of Genealogy Craze." https://www.usatoday.com/story/opinion/2014/05/12/genealogy-americans-technology-roots-porn-websites-column/9019409.

Rosenberg, Eli. "John Wayne." https://www.washingtonpost.com/arts-entertainment/2019/02/20/i-believe-white-supremacy-john-waynes-notorious-playboy-interview-goes-viral-twitter/?utm_term=.8a2bd16f9d3d.

Sacks, Jonathan. "The Book of the Covenant." (Devarim 5777.) http://rabbisacks.org/book-covenant-devarim-5777/.

———. *Covenant & Conversation: A Weekly Reading of the Jewish Bible, Genesis: The Book of Beginnings.* Jerusalem: Maggid, 2009.

———. *Essays on Ethics.* Jerusalem: Maggid, 2016.

———. "Spirituality of Listening." http://rabbisacks.org/spirituality-listening-ekev-5776/.

Sacks, Oliver. *Musicophilia: Tales of Music and the Brain.* New York: Vintage, 2008.

Schwarz, Alan. "Overcoming Addiction, Professor Tackles Perils American Indians Face." https://www.nytimes.com/2013/05/12/us/professor-ex-addict-confronts-perils-american-indians-aaface.html?pagewanted=all&_r=0.

Scienceinsanity.com. "World's First Human Head Transplant." http://www.scienceinsanity.com/2019/01/the-worlds-first-human-head-transplant.html

Smith, Christian. *Moral Believing Animals.* Oxford: Oxford University Press, 2003.

Smith, James K. A. *Desiring the Kingdom.* Grand Rapids: Baker Academic, 2009.

Spaemann, Robert. *Love and the Dignity of Human Life.* Grand Rapids: Eerdmans, 2012.

Spinoza, Benedict. *Ethics.* Ware, Hertfordshire: Wordsworth Edition Limited, 2001.

Theguardian.com. "Scientists debate ethics of human gene editing (Gene Splitting)." https://www.theguardian.com/science/2015/dec/01/human-gene-editing-international-summit.

Vaticannews.va. "Respect for the World Begins with the Human Body." https://www.vaticannews.va/en/pope/news/2018-06/pope-francis-general-assembly-pontifical-academy-for-life.html.

West, Ed. *1066 and Before All That.* Delaware: Skyhorse, 2017.

Wikipedia.org. "Alcohol and Native Americans." https://en.wikipedia.org/wiki/Alcohol_and_Native_Americans.

———. "Augustine of Hippo." https://en.wikipedia.org/wiki/Augustine_of_Hippo.

———. "Beat Generation." https://en.wikipedia.org/wiki/Beat_Generation.

———. "Crazy Horse." https://en.wikipedia.org/wiki/Crazy_Horse.

———. "Frankenstein." https://en.wikipedia.org/wiki/Frankenstein.

———. "Honor Killing." https://en.wikipedia.org/wiki/Honor_killiing.

————. "Honor Killing in Pakistan." https://en.wikipedia.org/wiki/Honour_killing_in_ Pakistan.

————. "Matrilineality." https://en.wikipedia.org/wiki/Matrilineality.

————. "Matrilineality in Judaism." https://en.wikipedia.org/w/index.php?title= Matrilineality_in_Judaism&oldid=894226422.

————. "A rose by any other name would smell as sweet." https://en.wikipedia.org/ wiki/A_rose_by_any_other_name_would_smell_as_sweet.

————. "The Selfish Gene." https://en.m.wikipedia.org/wiki/The_Selfish_Gene.

————. "True Name." https://en.wikipedia.org/wiki, /True name.

————. "Tsutomu Yamaguchi." https://en.wikipedia.org/wiki/Tsutomu_Yamaguchi.

————. "Yin Yang." https://en.wikipedia.org/wiki/Yin_and_yang.

Wilson, Edward O. *The Meaning of Human Existence*. New York: Liveright, 2014.

Windhorst, Brian. "Kyrie Irving." http://www.espn.com/nba/story/_/id/24454604/kyrie-irving-boston-celtics-gets-little-mountain-lakota-name-standing-rock-sioux-tribe.

Wooden, John, with Jay Carty. *Coach Wooden's Pyramid of Success*. Grand Rapids: Revell, 2009.

Worrall, Simon. "Why Race is Not a Thing According to Genetics." https://news.nationalgeographic.com/2017/10/genetics-history-race-neanderthal-rutherford/.

Yetman, Norman R. *Voices from Slavery*. Mineola, NY: Dover, 1999.

Youtube.com. "Meet the Woman Who Learned that Her Mother Passed for White." https://www.youtube.com/watch?v=oNiEBnOzgVw.

————. "Muhammad Ali vs. Ernie Terrell." https://www.youtube.com/watch?v=-TJbjS2mdJE&t=77s.

————. "Open Marriage Ends Tragically." https://www.youtube.com/watch? v=RLxYxzPoqX8.

————. "The Family that Walks on All Fours." https://www.youtube.com/watch? v=Jwiz-yhLpTo.